# HARAJUKU
## DRESS TO IMPRESS

**Written and imagined by Mika Harada**

# Harajuku Dress to Impress

© 2024 Mika Harada

All rights reserved. Yes, that means you can't photocopy, scan, or share this book in any sneaky way without our permission. Piracy isn't fashionable, but asking nicely is always in style.

**Disclaimer:** No virtual models were overworked in the making of this book—though our computers might have pulled a few all-nighters.

This book is not just pages with pictures; it's a curated explosion of style straight from the vibrant streets of Harajuku. The images inside were brought to life using some seriously advanced AI wizardry. But don't be fooled—each image is the result of a creative journey filled with imagination, countless tweaks, and a whole lot of passion to capture the true essence of Harajuku fashion.

So dive in, get inspired, and maybe even start your own fashion revolution. Just remember, if you suddenly feel the urge to rock a neon tutu with combat boots, we're totally here for it.

**Published by Mika Harada**

**First Edition**

# INTRODUCTION

Welcome to the Vibrant World of Harajuku Fashion!

Step into the kaleidoscope of colors, patterns, and creativity that is Harajuku fashion—a style revolution born in the bustling streets of Tokyo's Harajuku district. Nestled between Shinjuku and Shibuya, Harajuku has long been a melting pot of culture, art, and youthful expression. In the aftermath of World War II, this area transformed into a hub where Western influences mingled with traditional Japanese aesthetics, giving rise to a unique fashion scene that defies conventions.

This book is your passport to a realm where self-expression knows no bounds and every outfit tells a story. Harajuku fashion is more than just clothing; it's a celebration of individuality and a fearless embrace of the unconventional. From the whimsical pastels of **Fairy Kei** to the bold elegance of **Gothic Lolita**, the styles captured in these pages showcase how fashion becomes an art form. Boys and girls alike turn the streets into their personal runways, blending elements like kimono fabrics, punk accessories, and vintage finds into looks that are entirely their own.

As you turn each page, you'll delve into the rich tapestry of Tokyo's fashion culture, deeply rooted in the spirit of Harajuku. The district's iconic **Takeshita Street** is lined with boutiques, cafes, and street vendors, all contributing to an atmosphere that encourages creativity and experimentation. Here, fashion isn't dictated by magazines or runways but is a living, breathing entity shaped by the people who wear it.

Harajuku's influence stretches far beyond its streets, inspiring global trends and challenging traditional notions of style. It's a place where subcultures thrive—where styles like Decora, adorned with colorful accessories, and Visual Kei, inspired by rock music, coexist and evolve. This melting pot of fashion fosters a community that values diversity, inclusivity, and the freedom to be oneself.

This collection isn't just about admiring stunning photographs—it's an invitation to ignite your imagination. Discover how the vibrant roots of Tokyo's fashion culture can inspire you to explore and define your own unique aesthetic. Let the eclectic styles and spirited energy of Harajuku encourage you to experiment with your wardrobe, embrace your quirks, and most importantly, be unapologetically you.

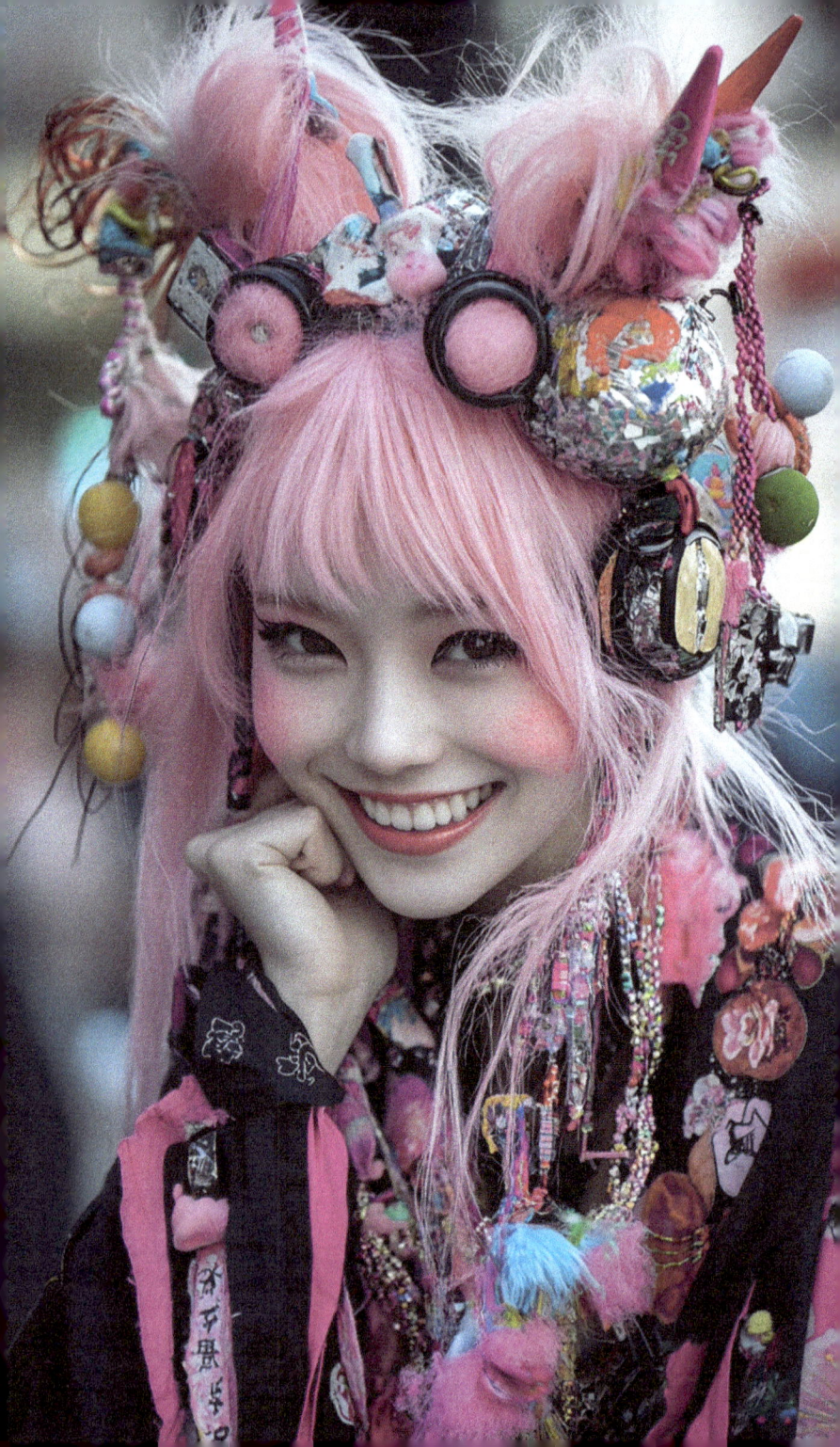

Harajuku's influence stretches far beyond its streets, inspiring global trends and challenging traditional notions of style. It's a place where subcultures thrive—where styles like Decora, adorned with colorful accessories, and Visual Kei, inspired by rock music, coexist and evolve. This melting pot of fashion fosters a community that values diversity, inclusivity, and the freedom to be oneself.

This collection isn't just about admiring stunning photographs—it's an invitation to ignite your imagination. Discover how the vibrant roots of Tokyo's fashion culture can inspire you to explore and define your own unique aesthetic. Let the eclectic styles and spirited energy of Harajuku encourage you to experiment with your wardrobe, embrace your quirks, and most importantly, be unapologetically you.

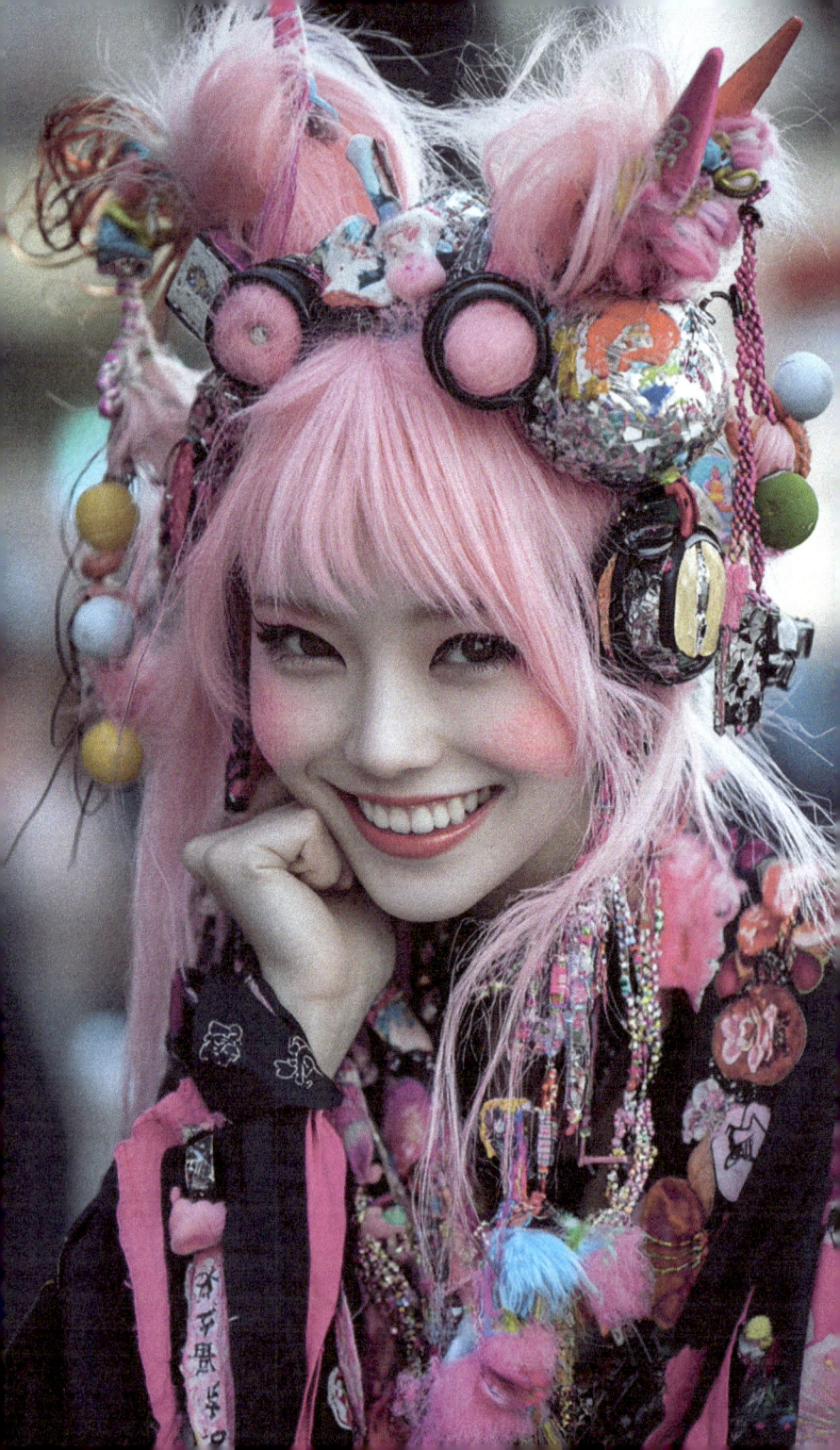

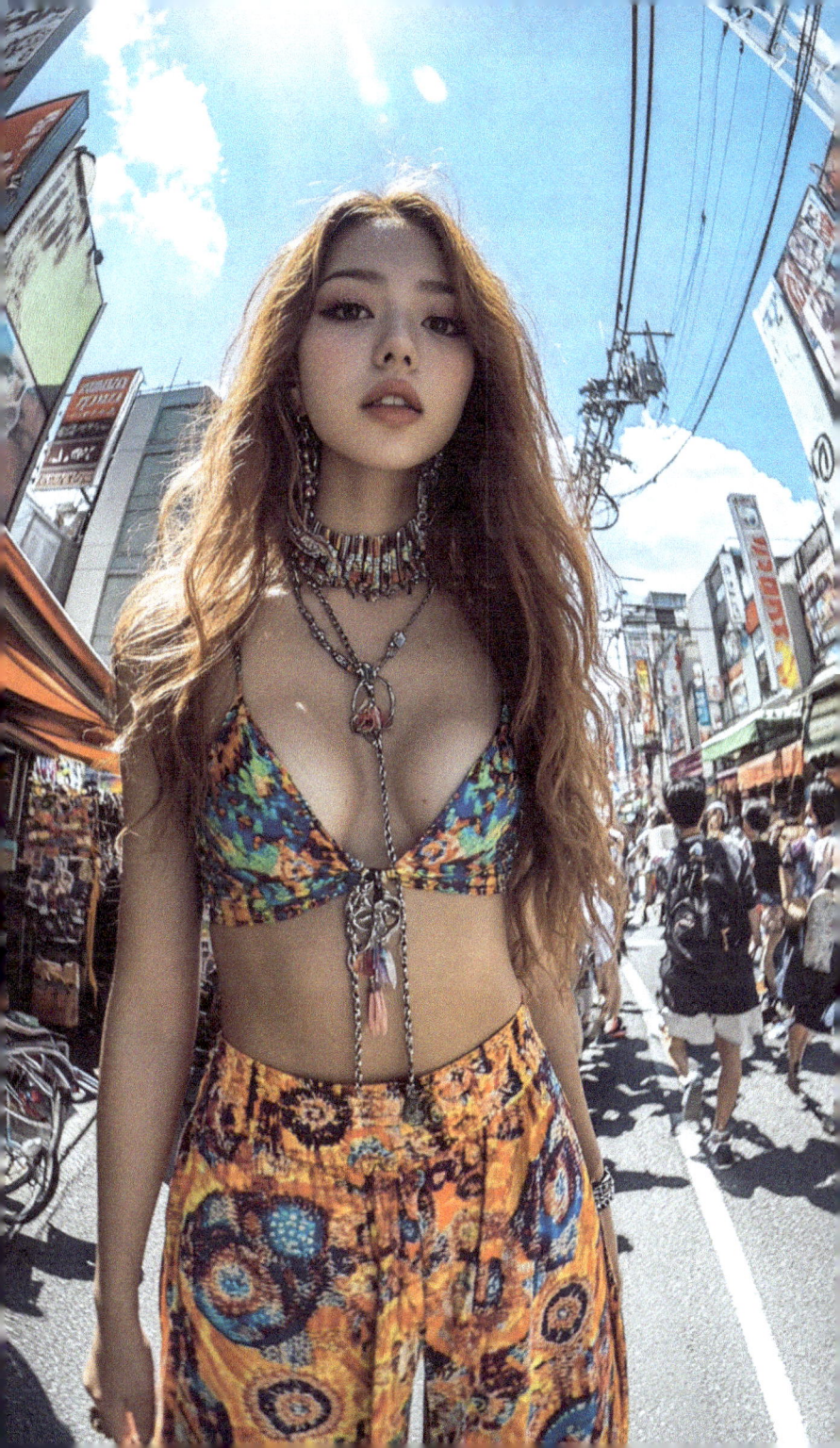

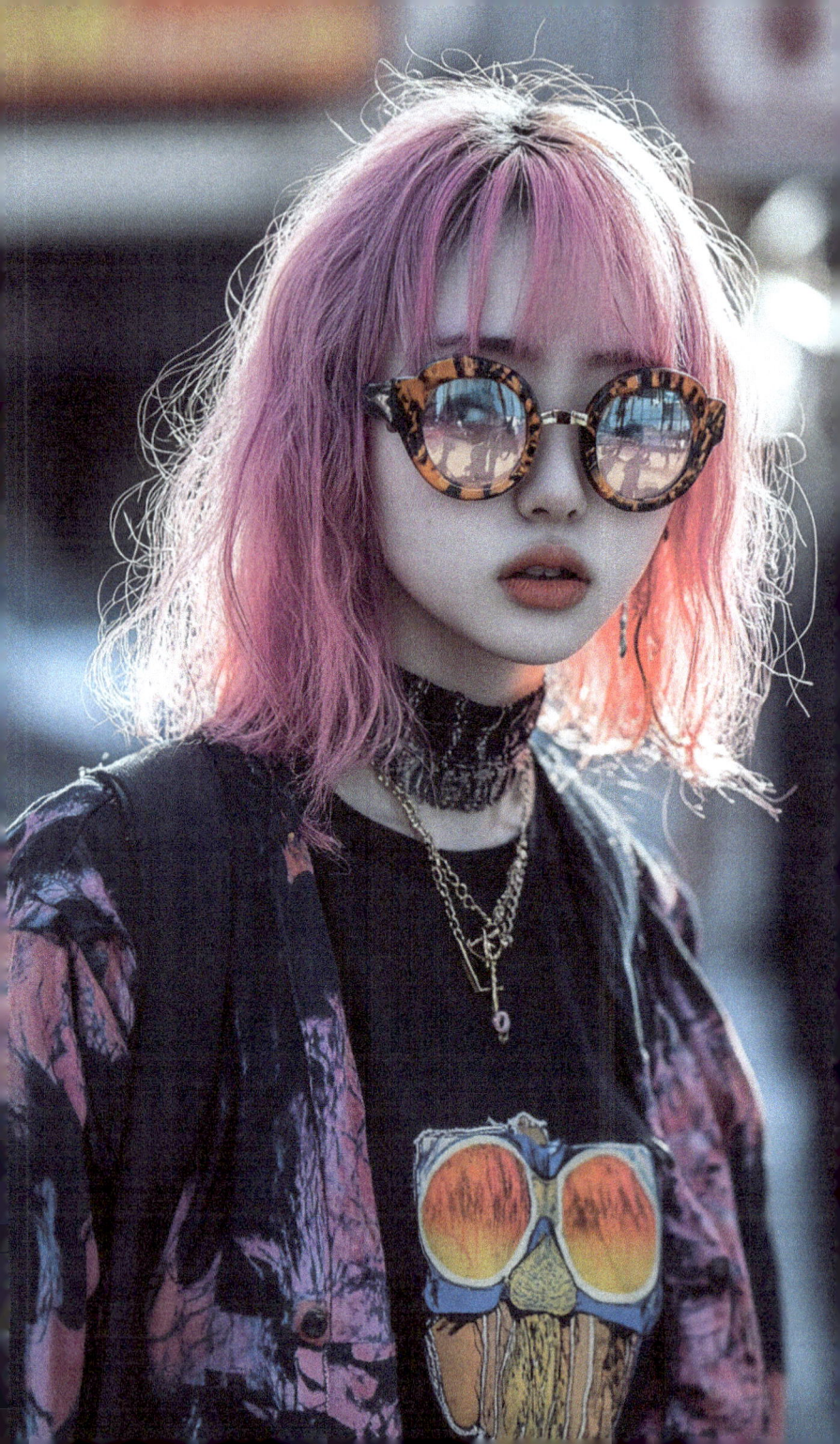

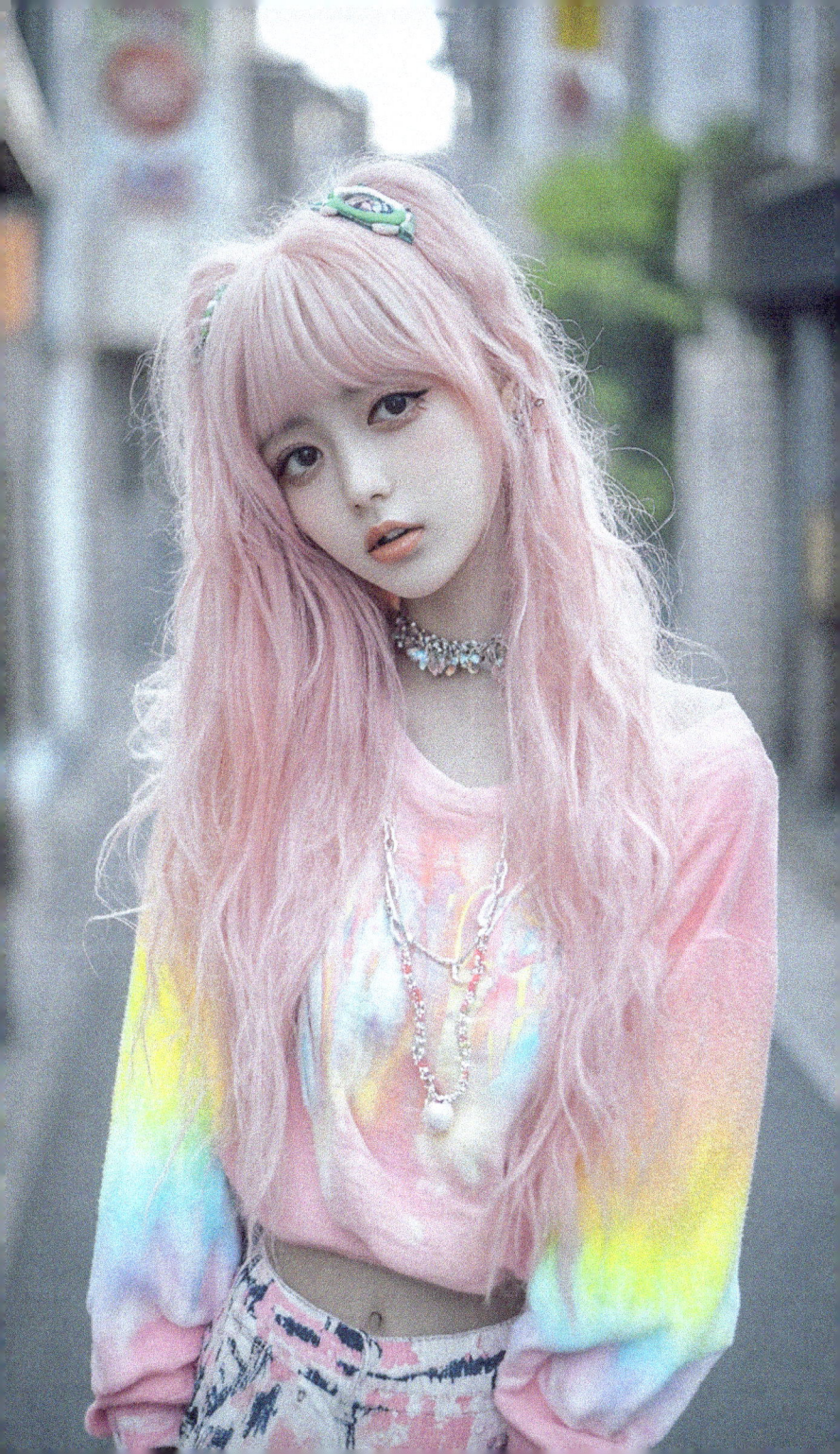

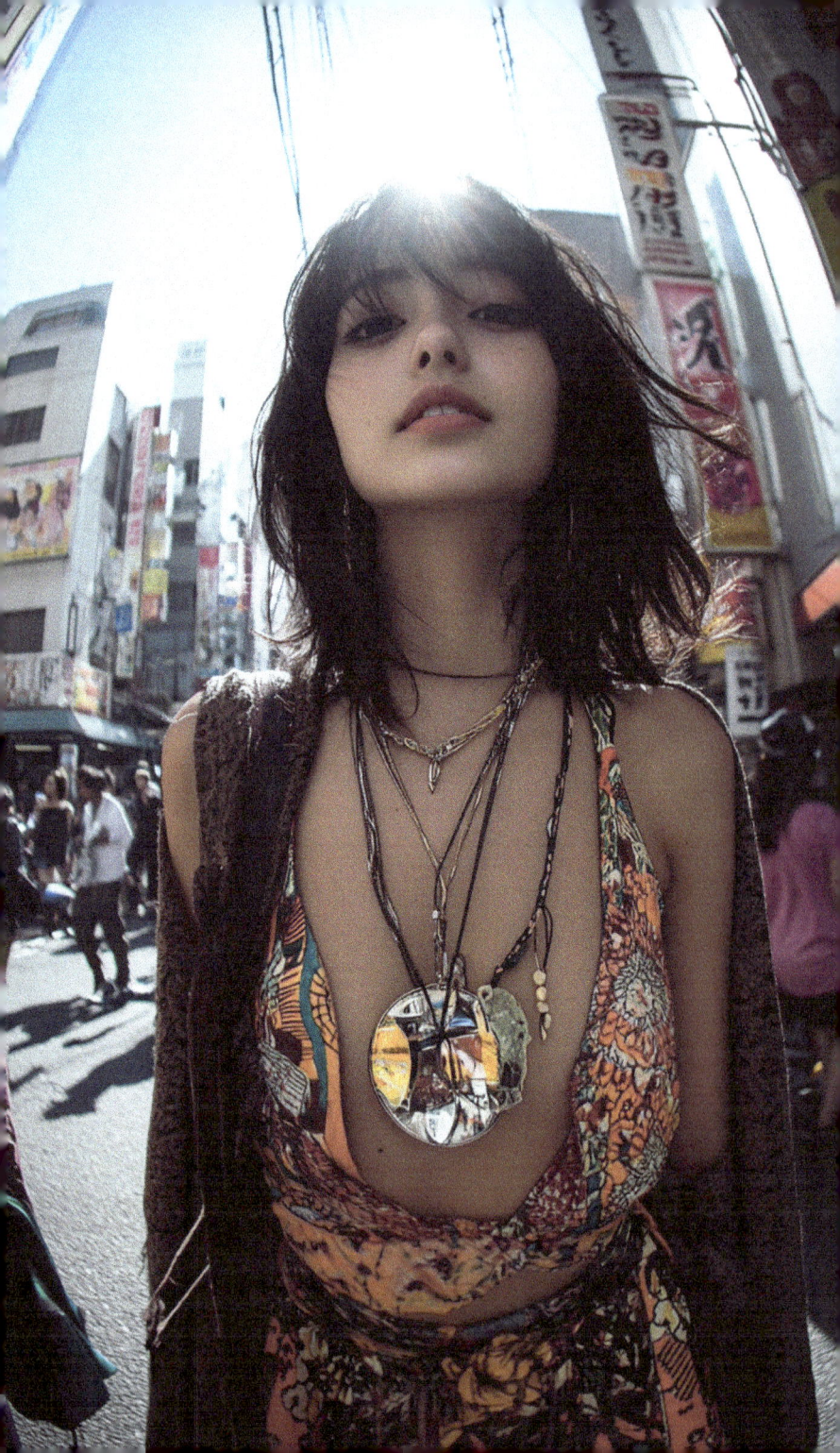

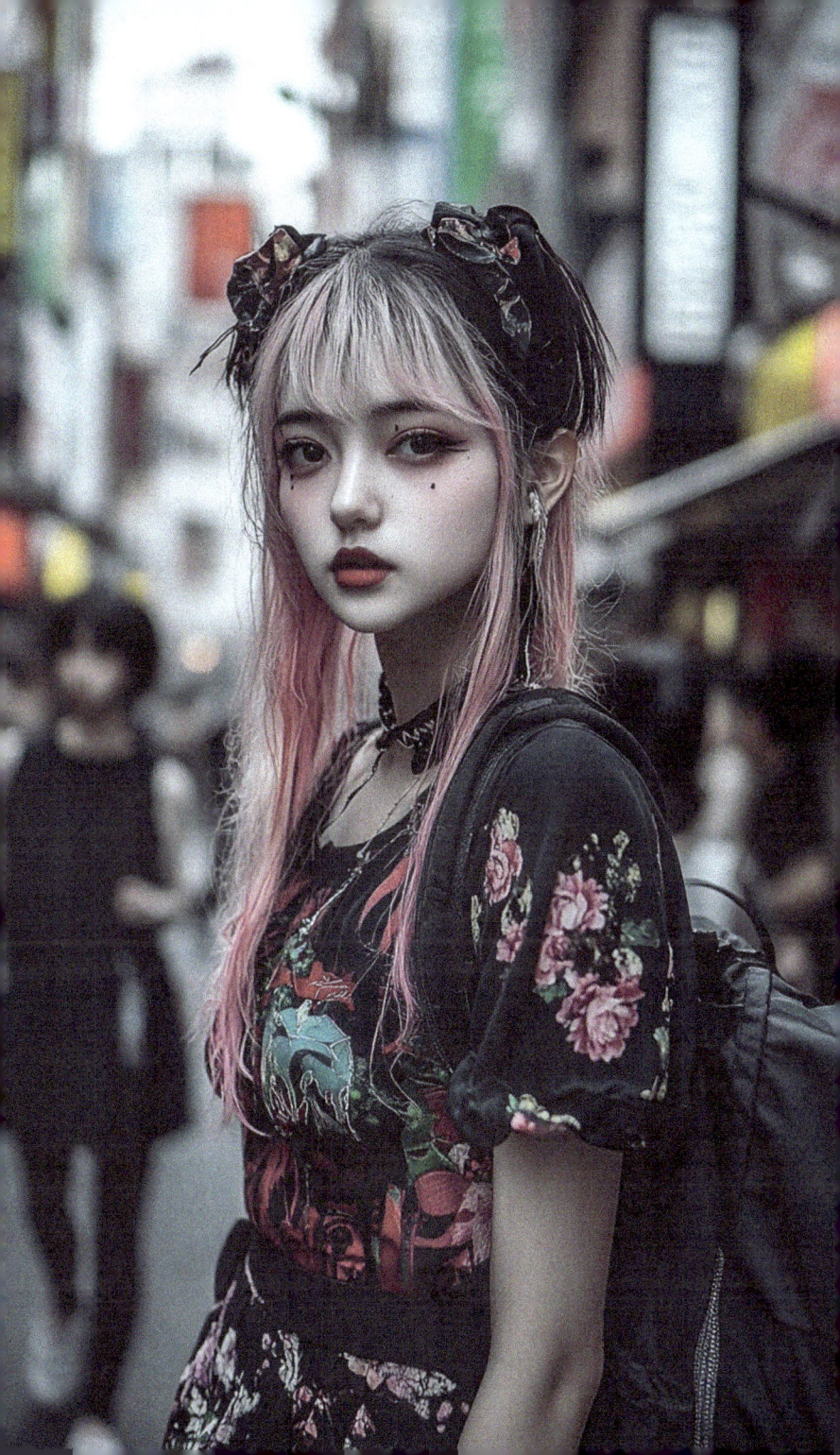

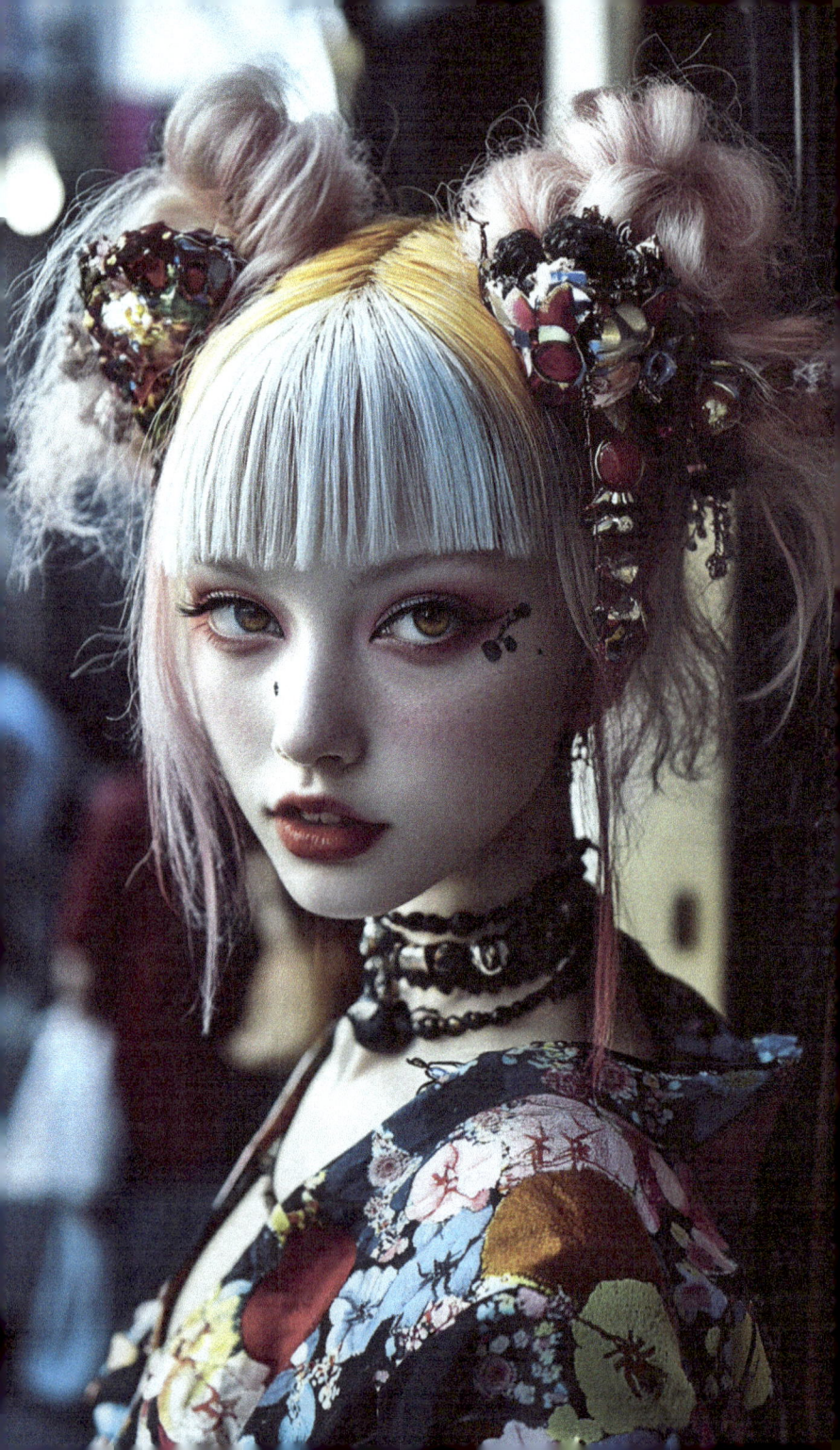

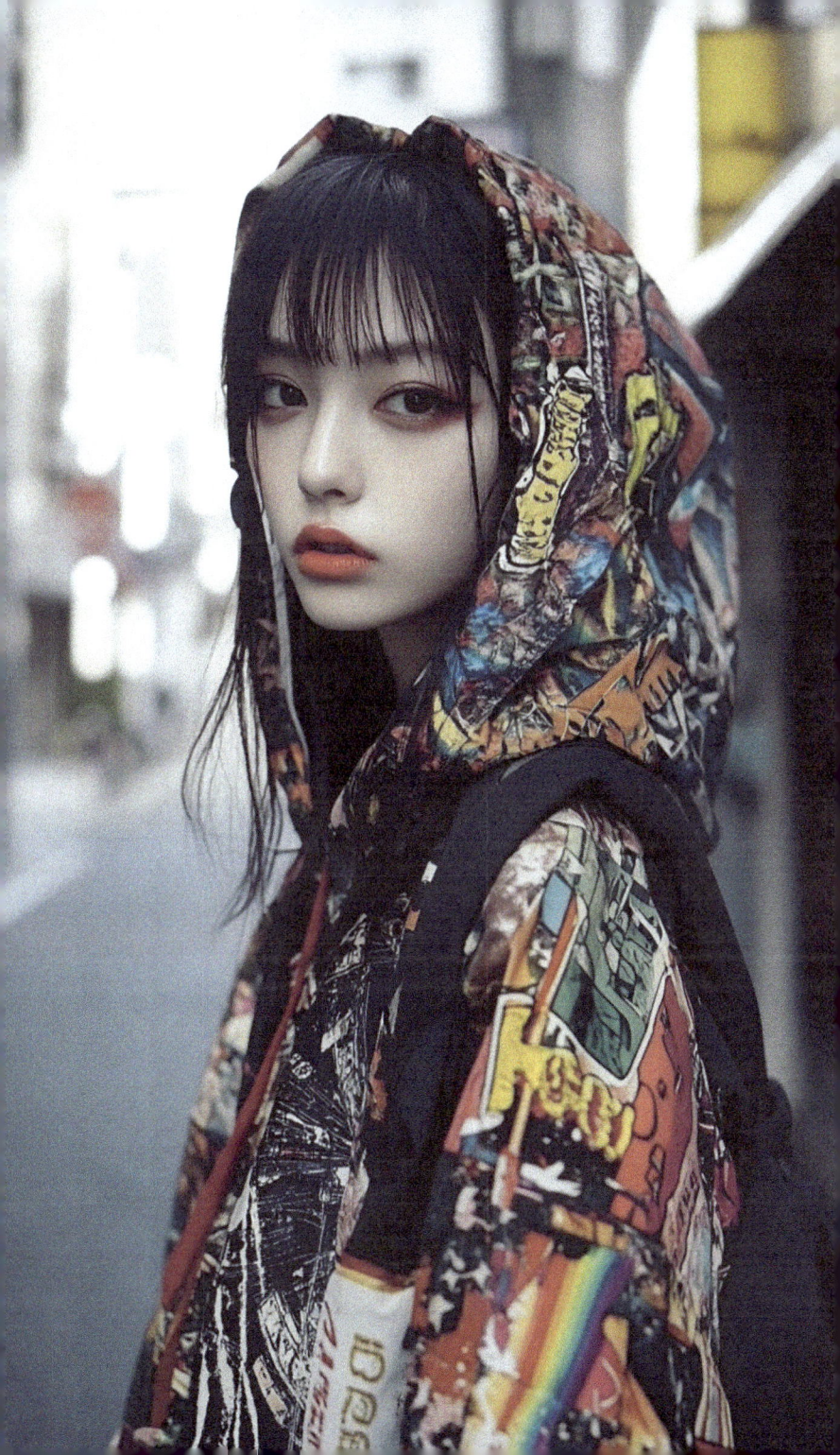

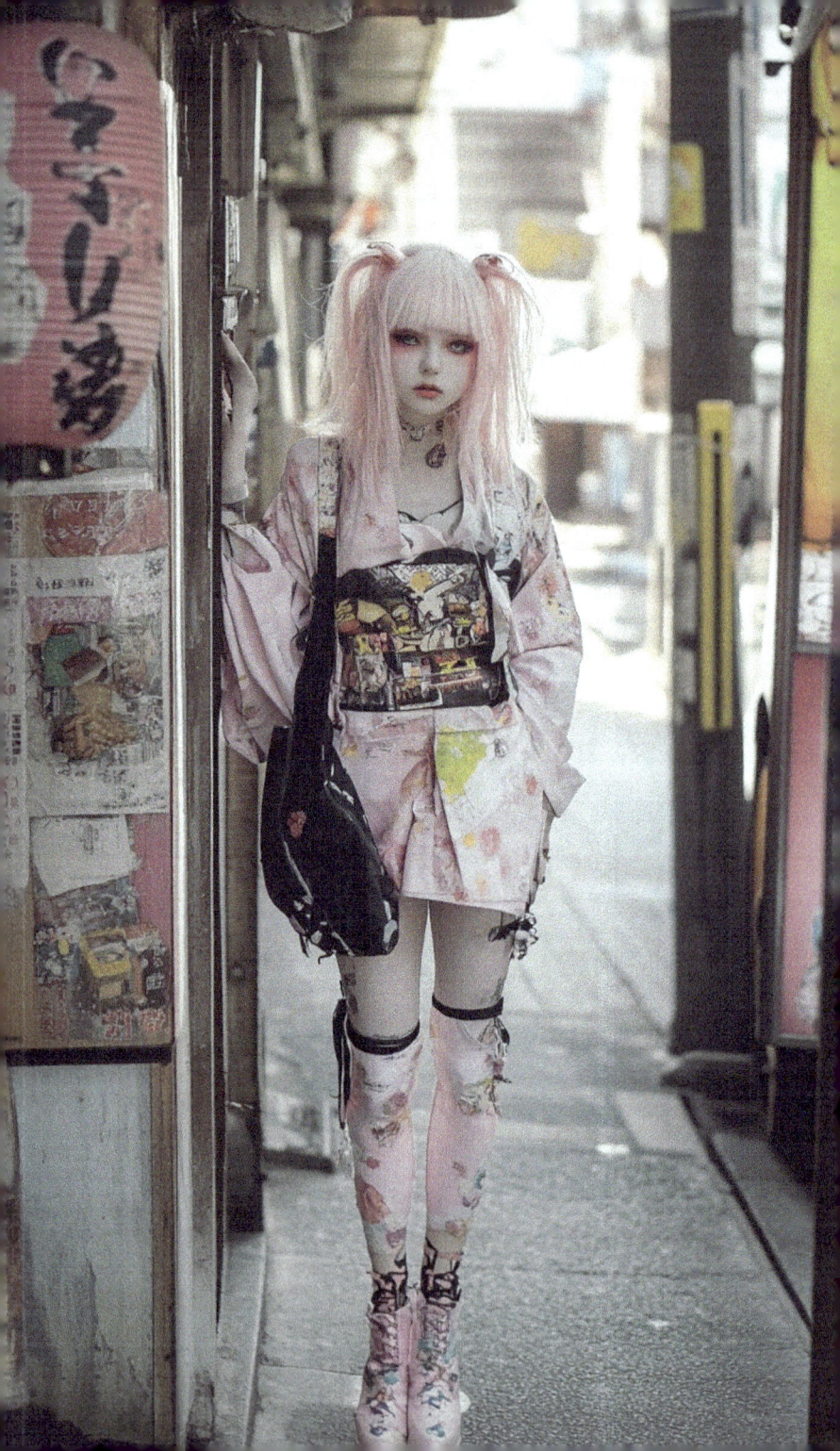

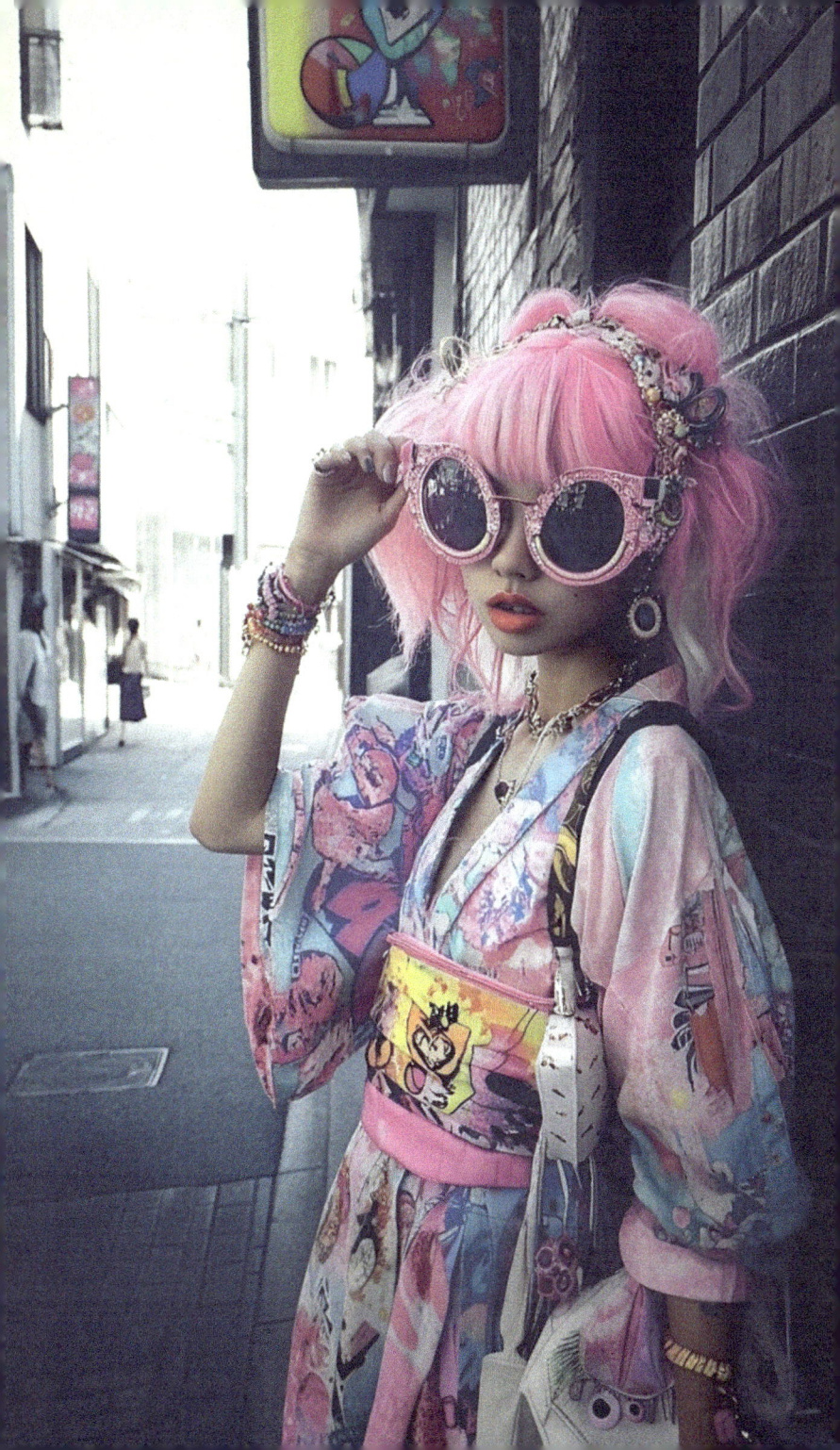

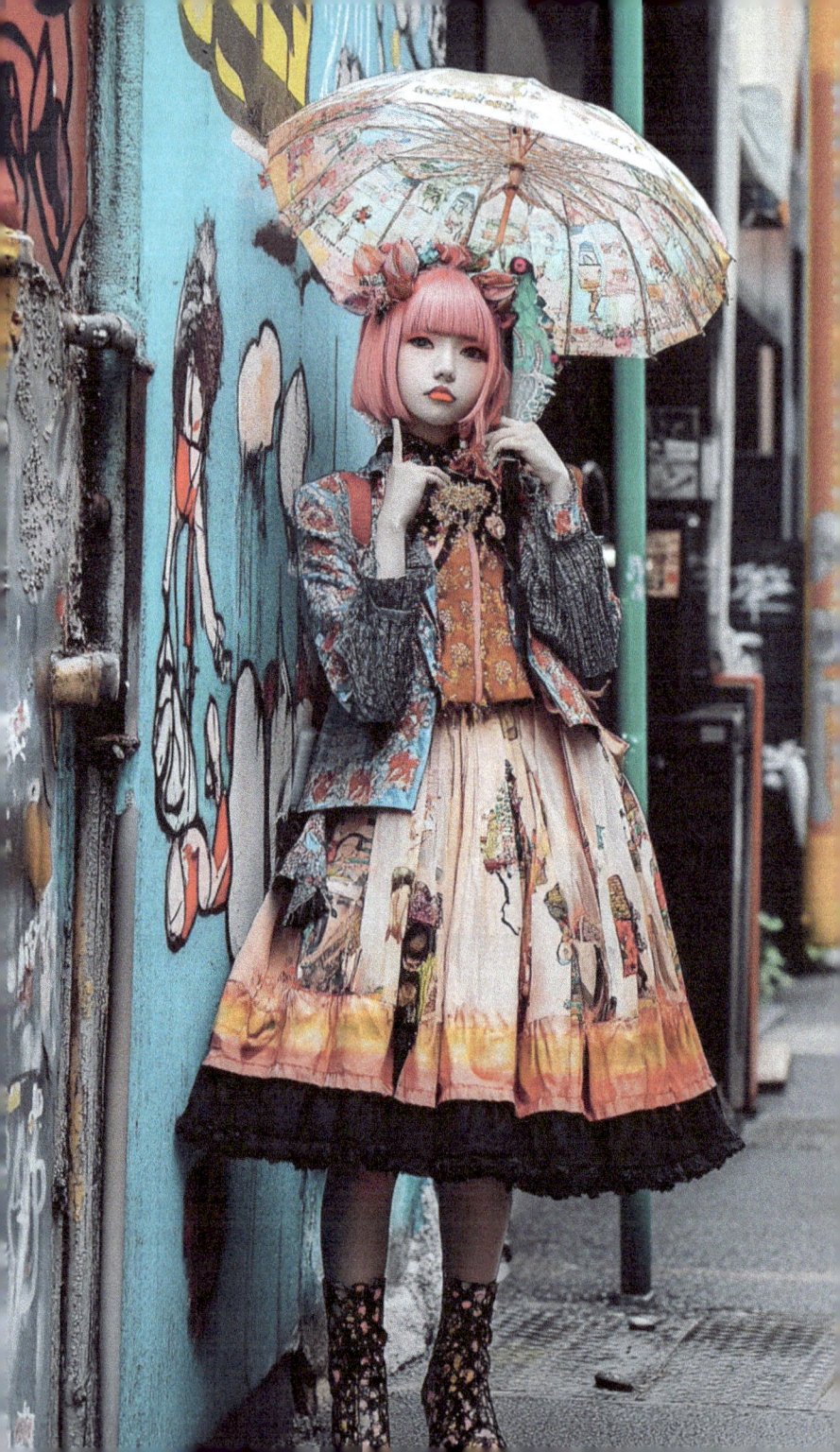

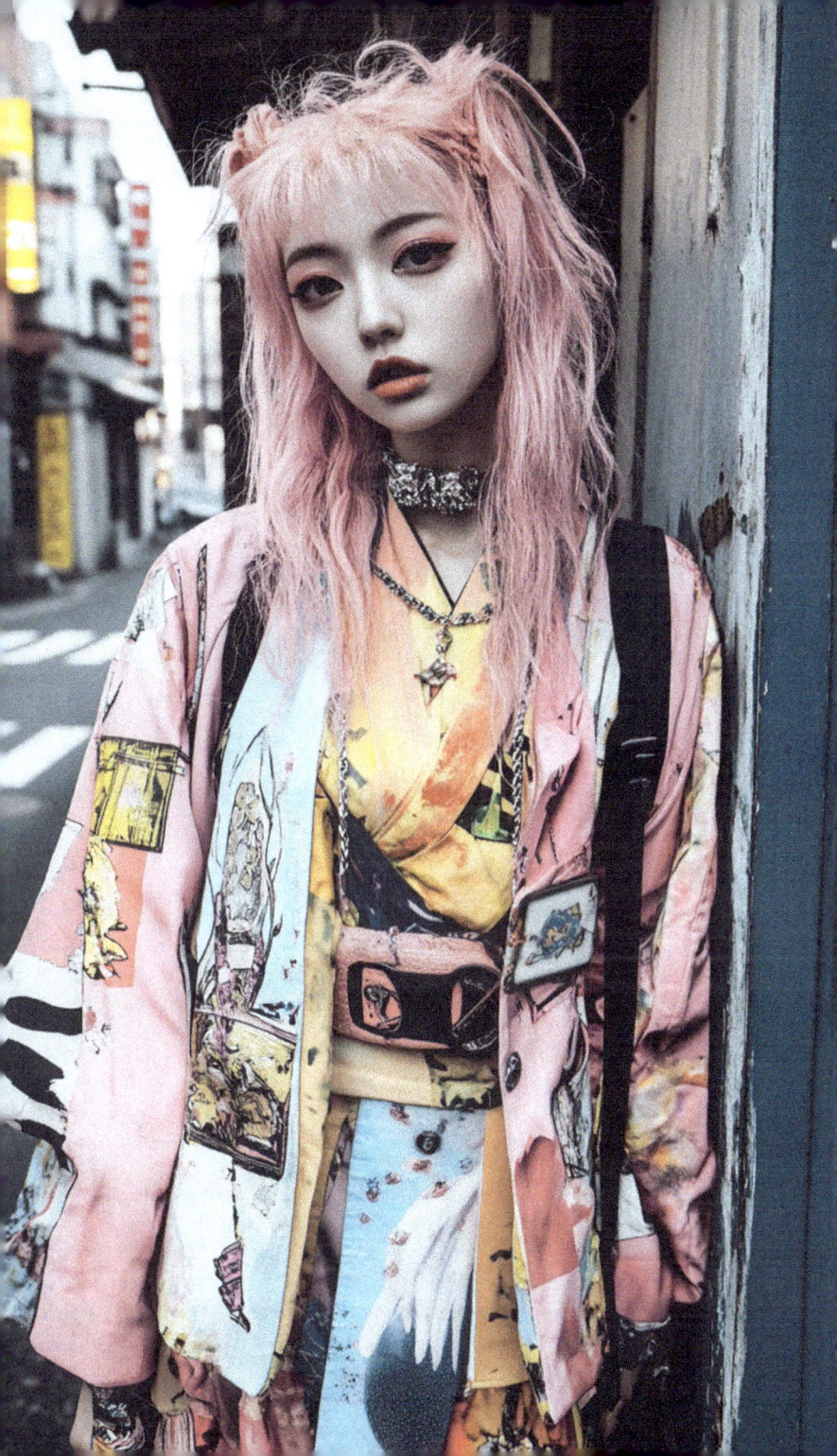

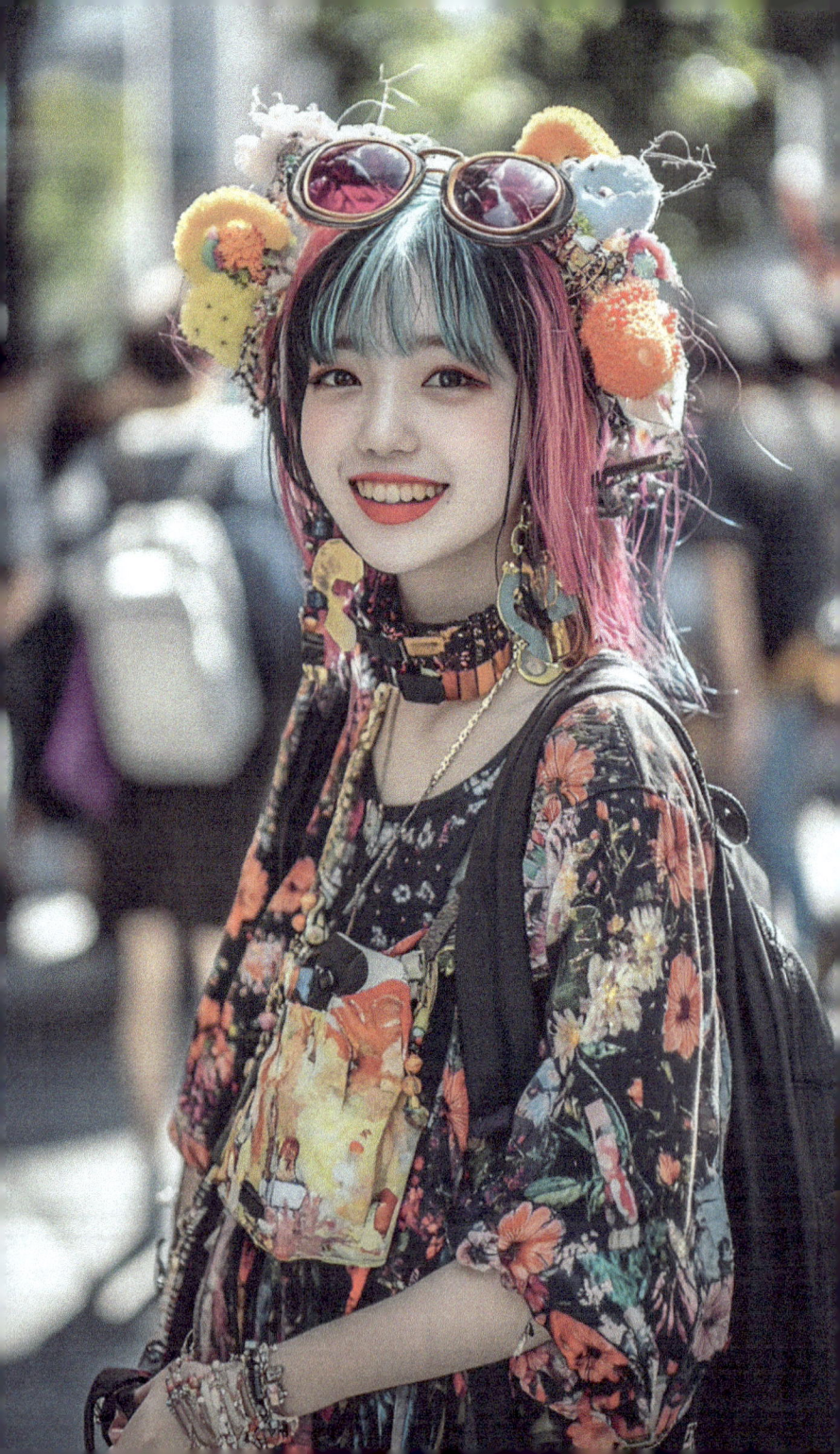

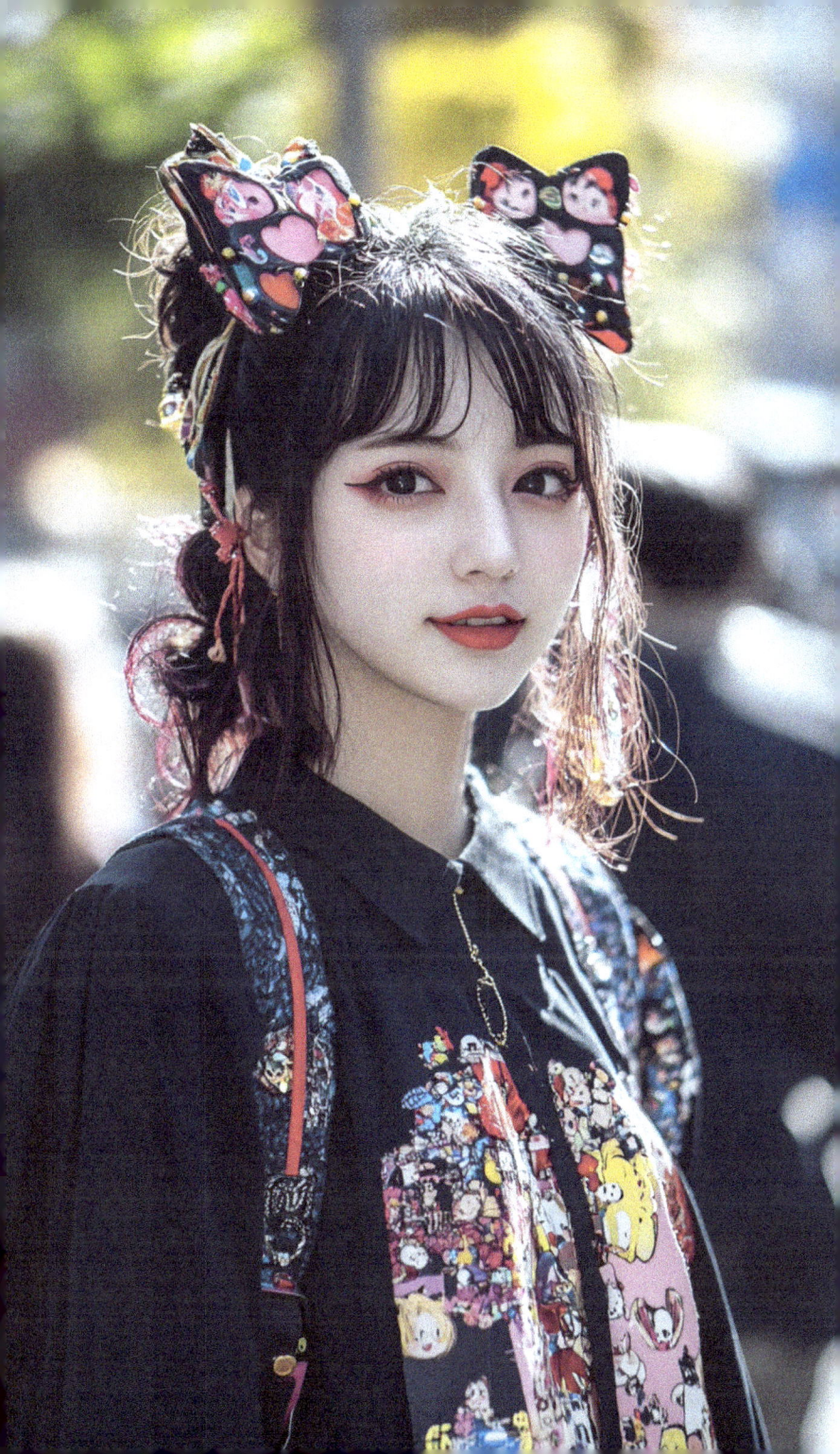

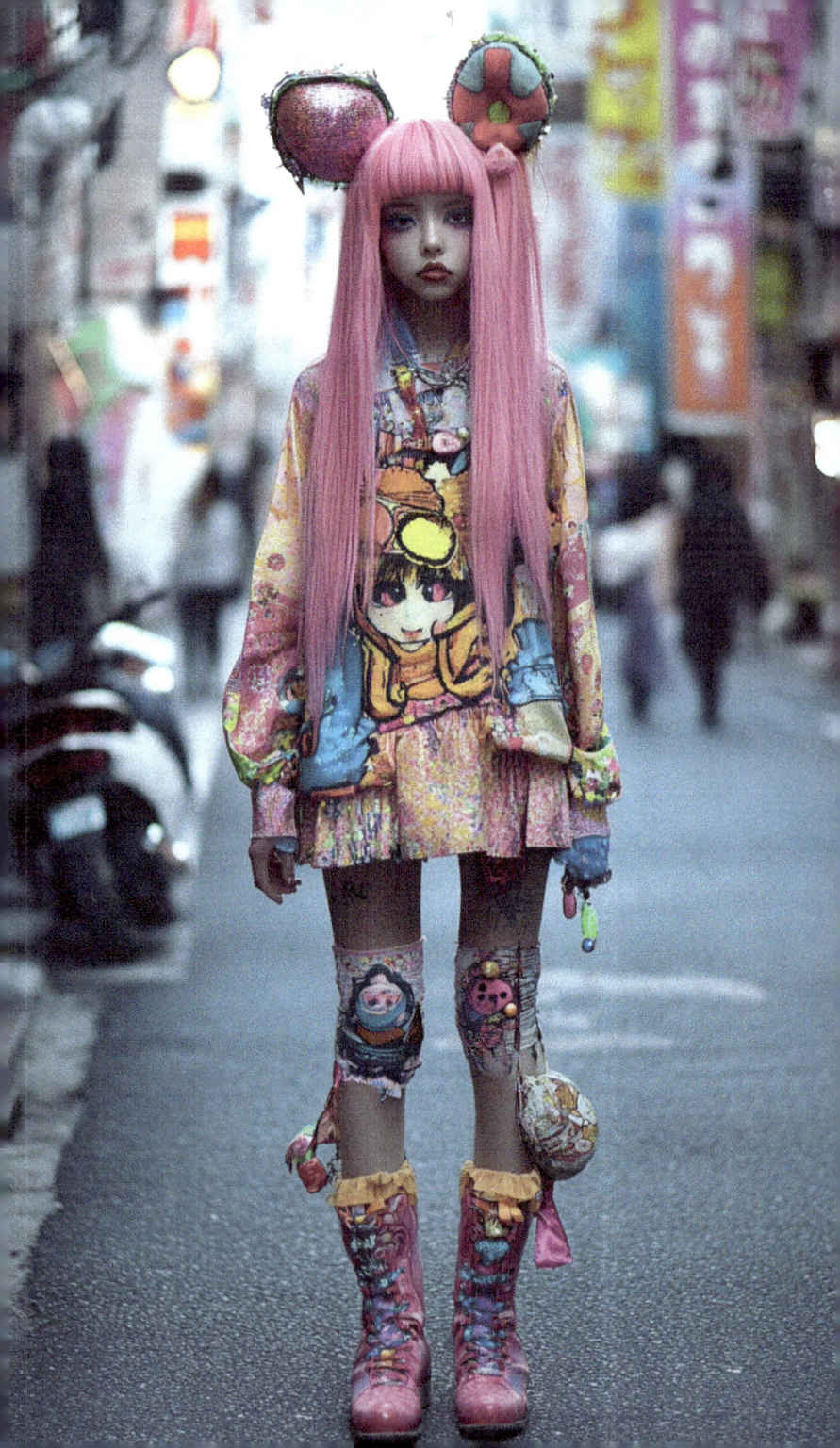

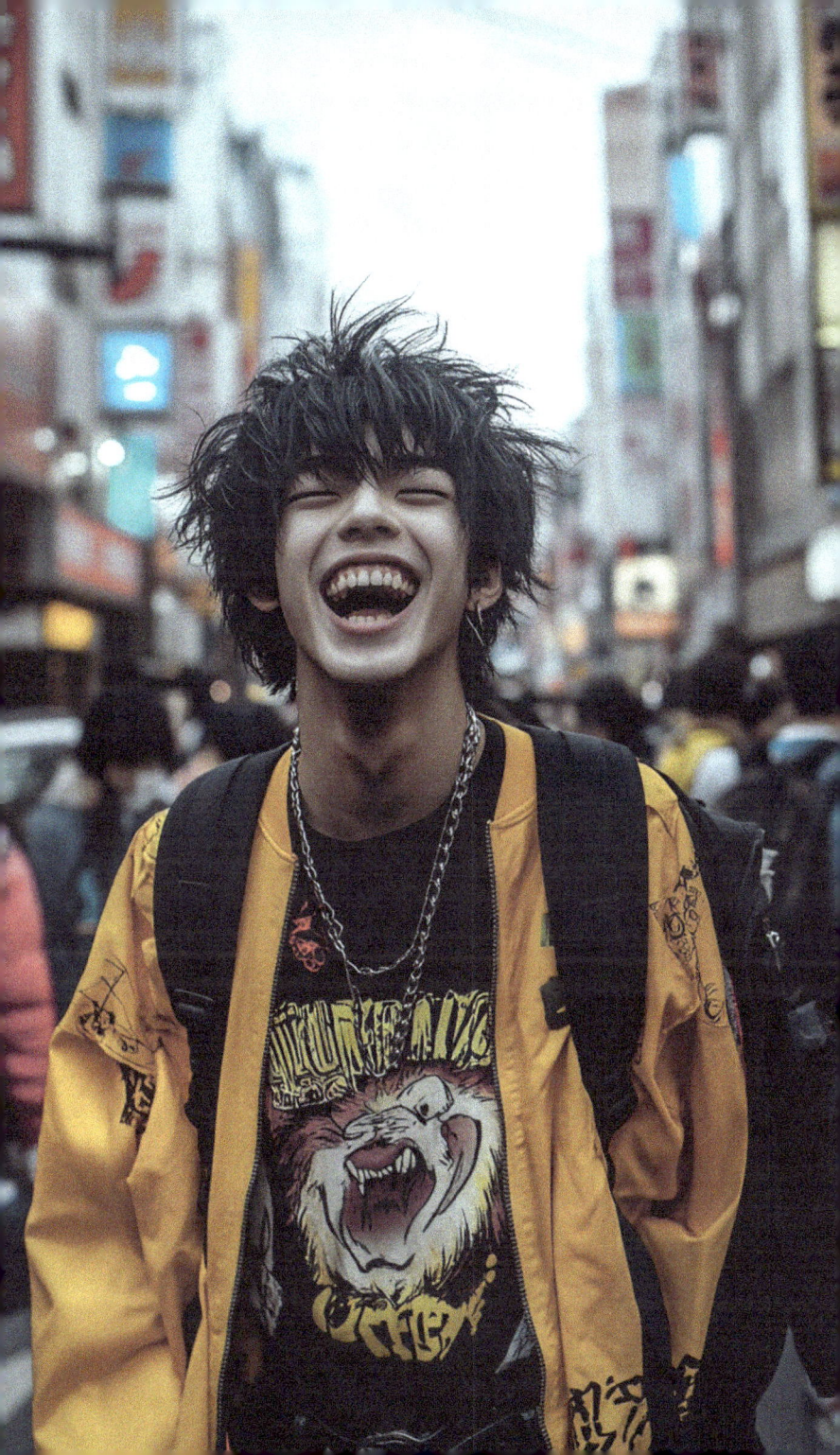

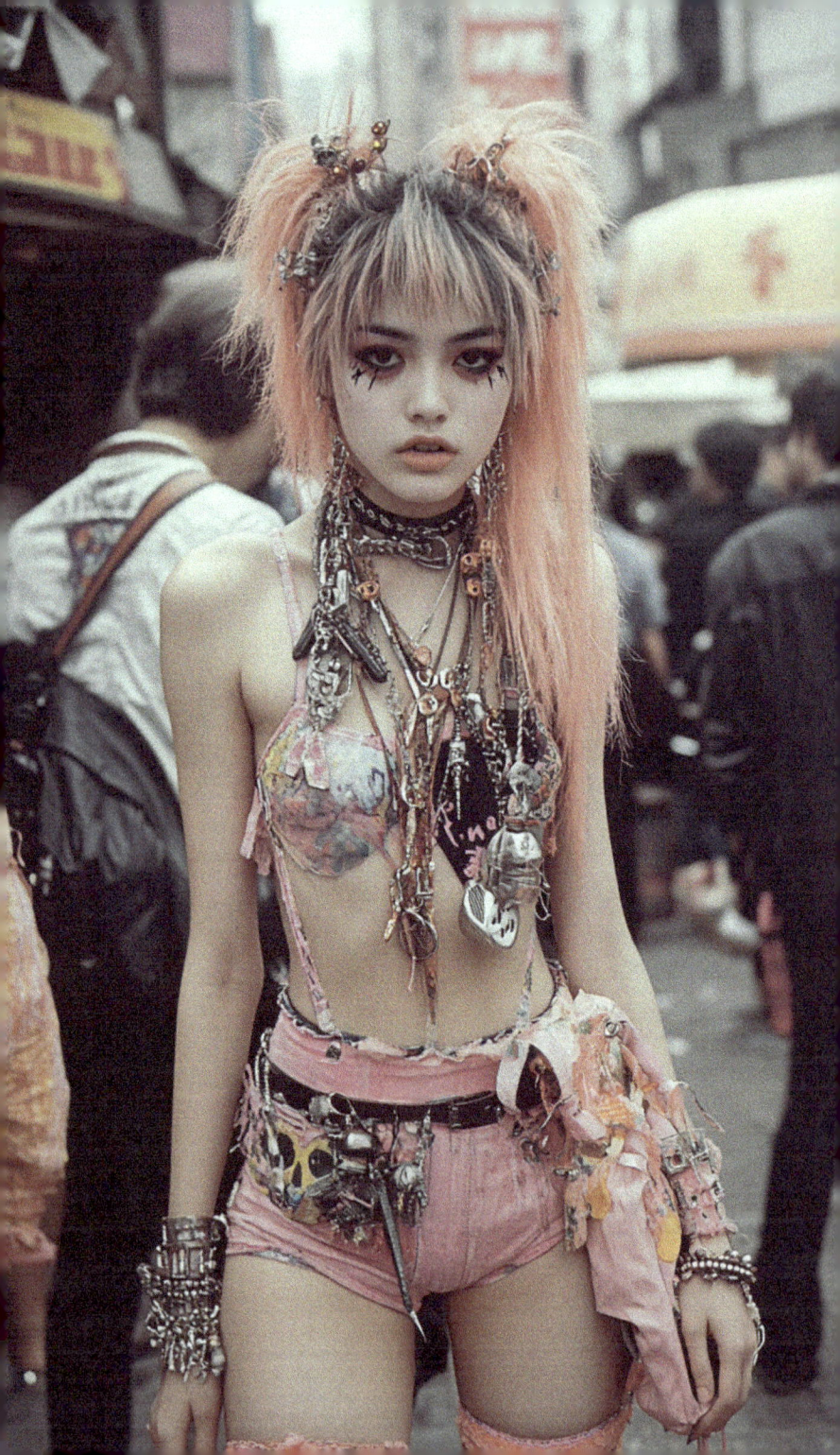

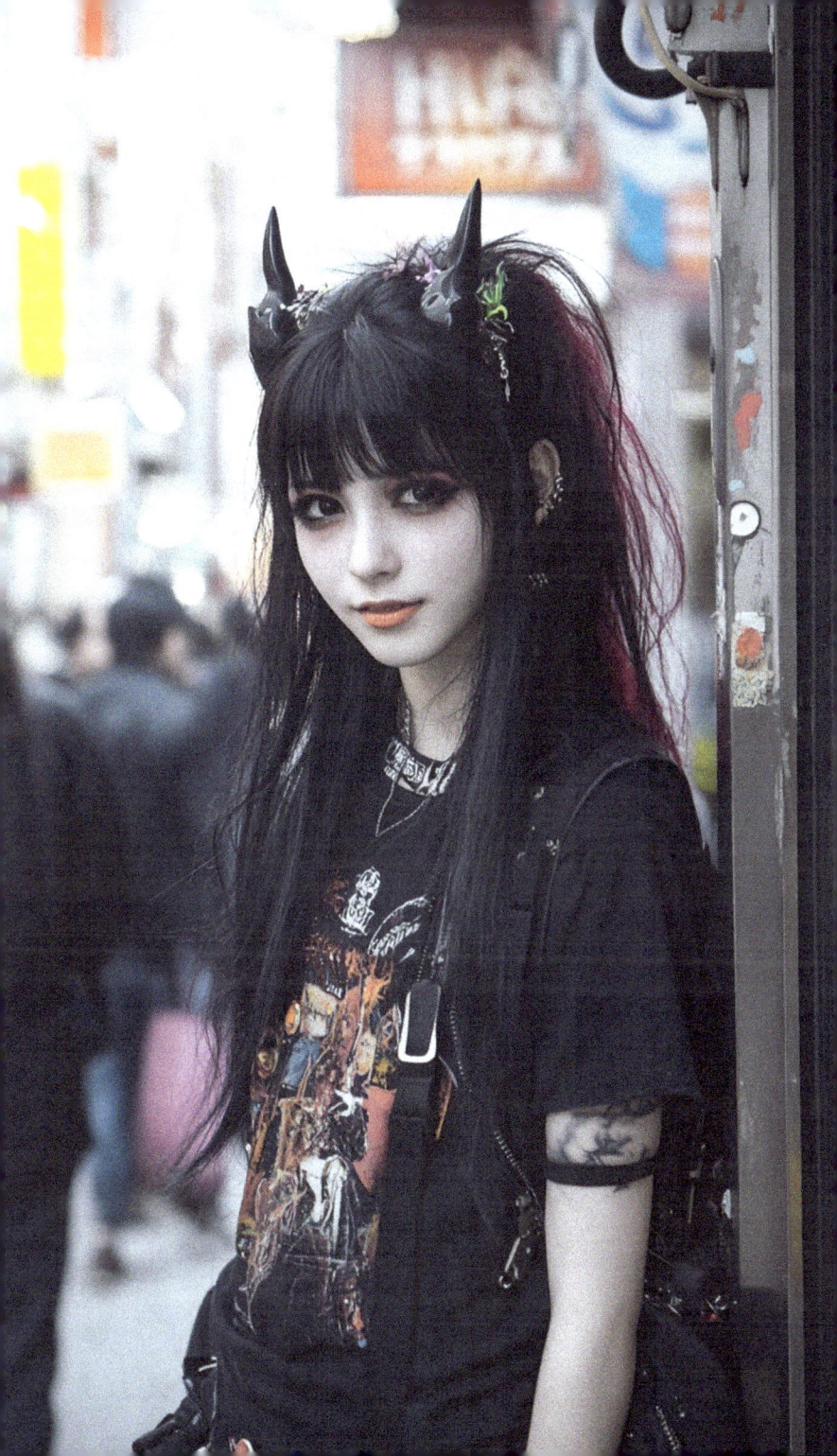

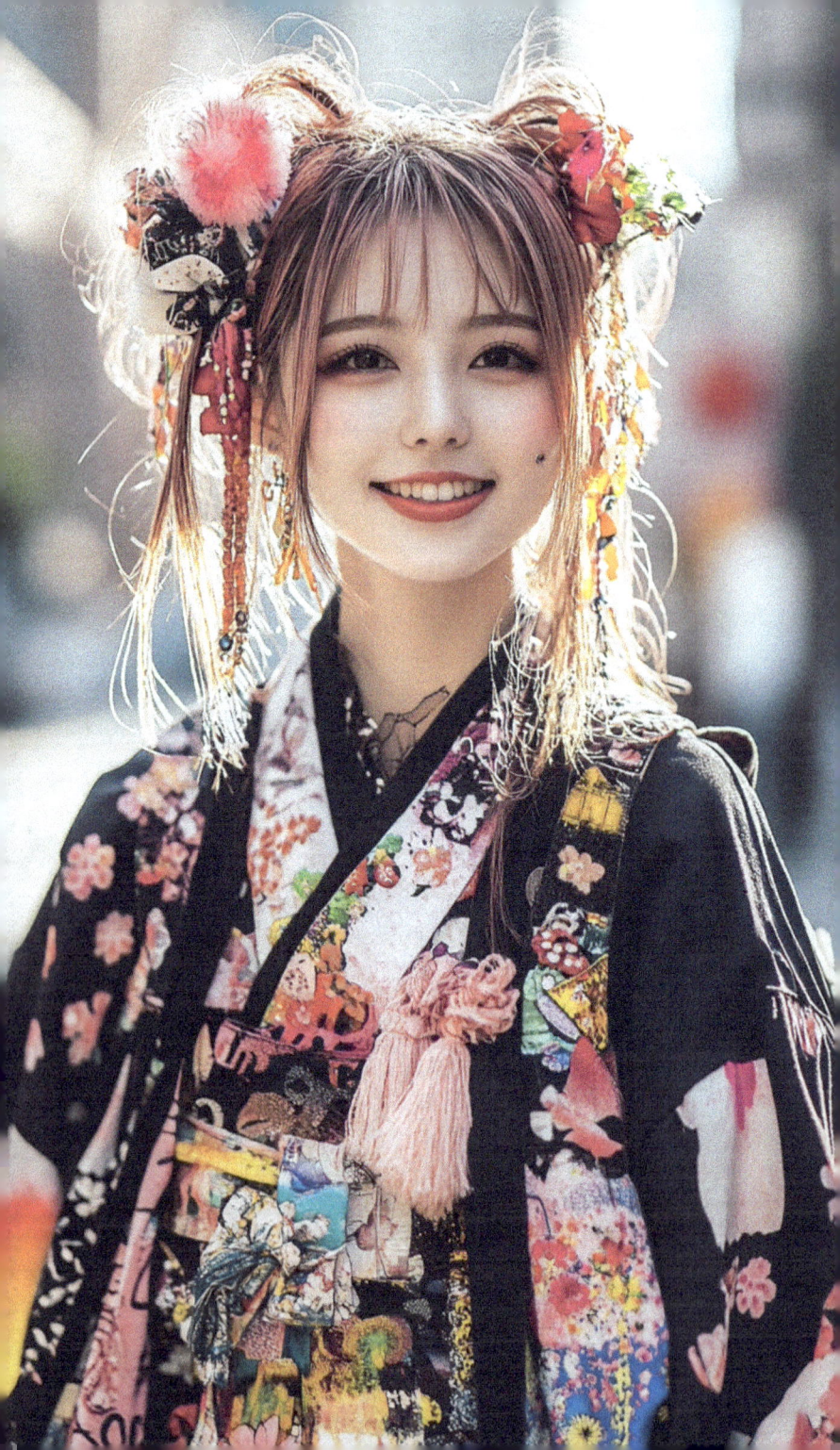

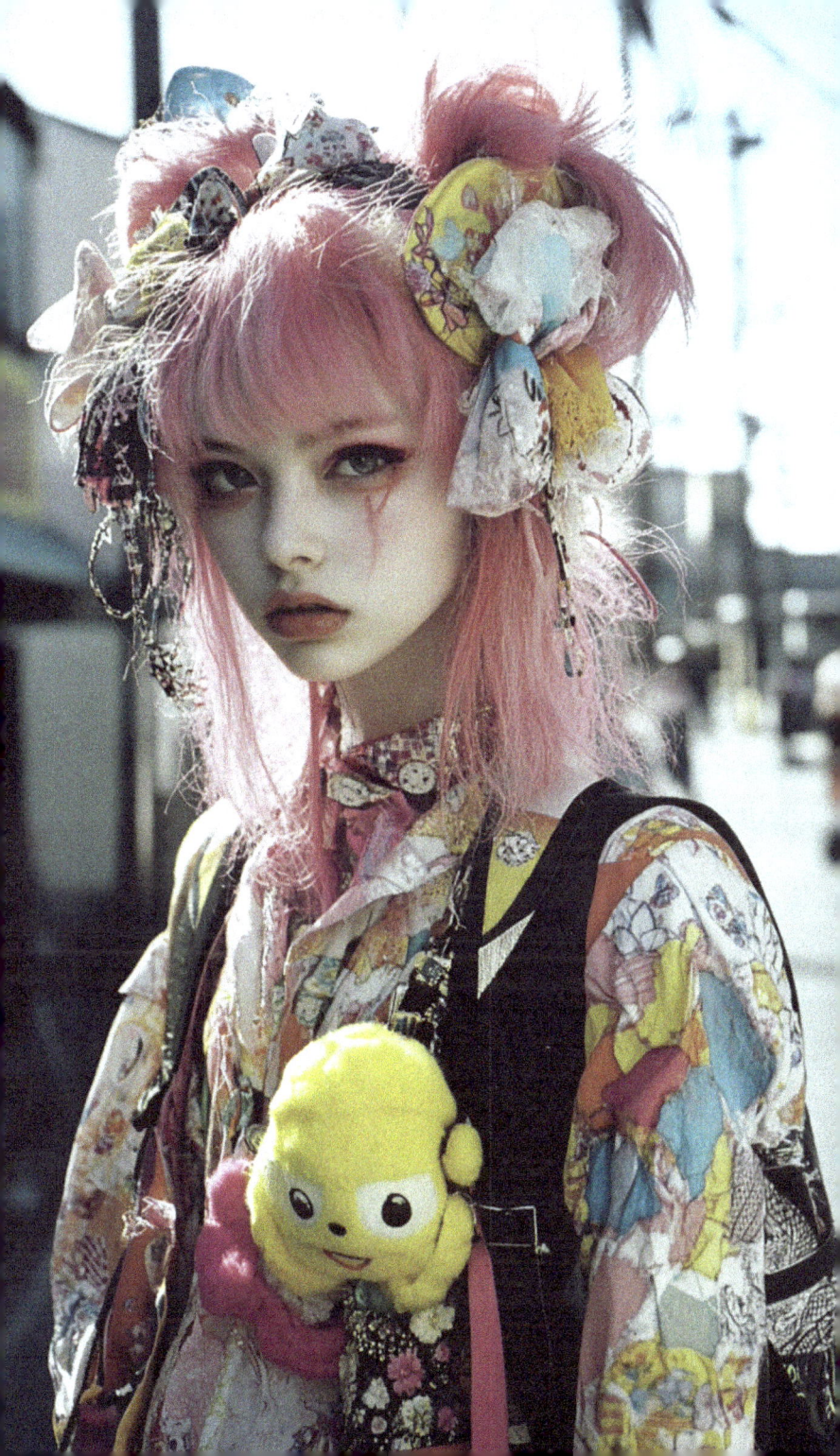

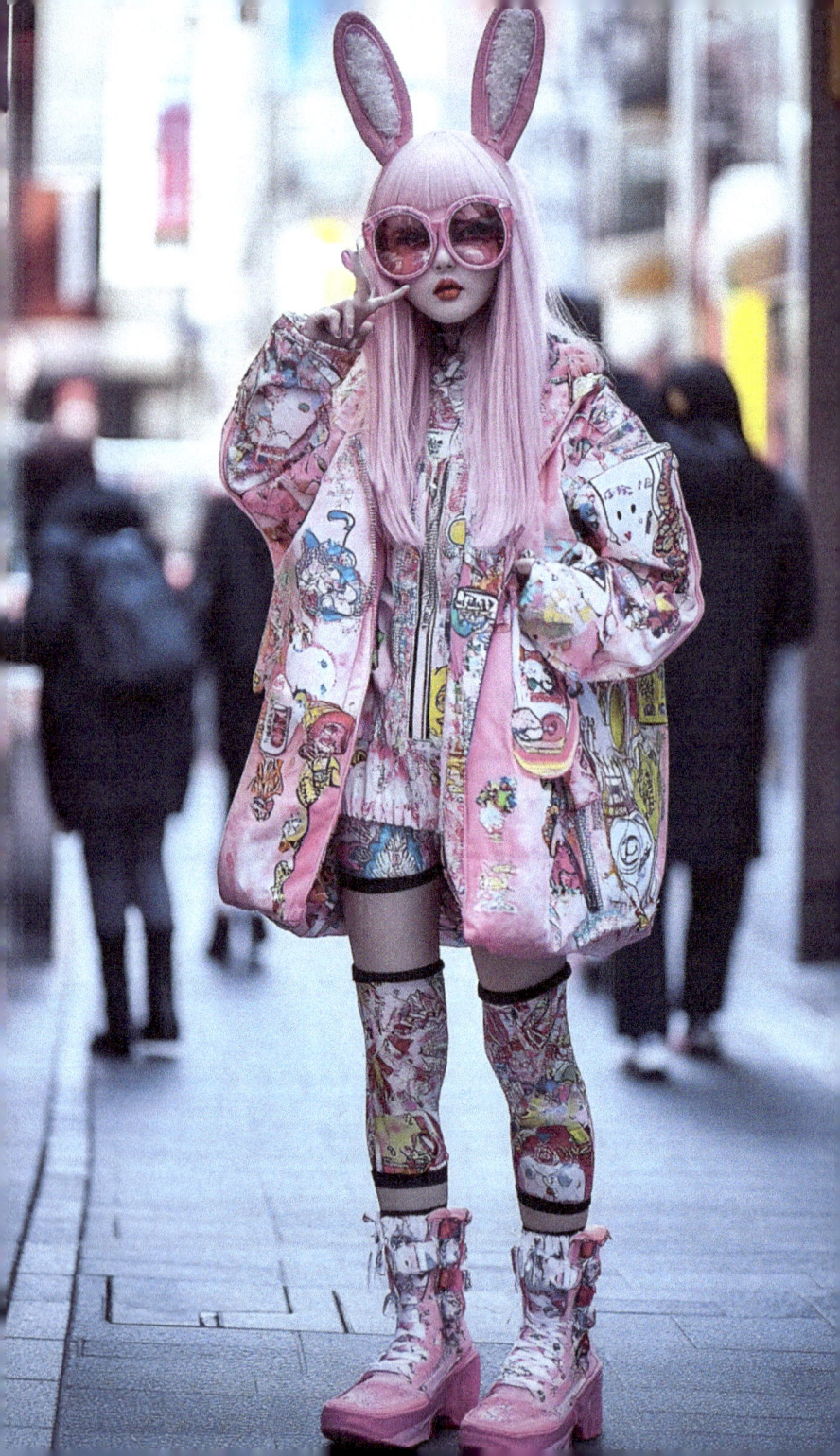

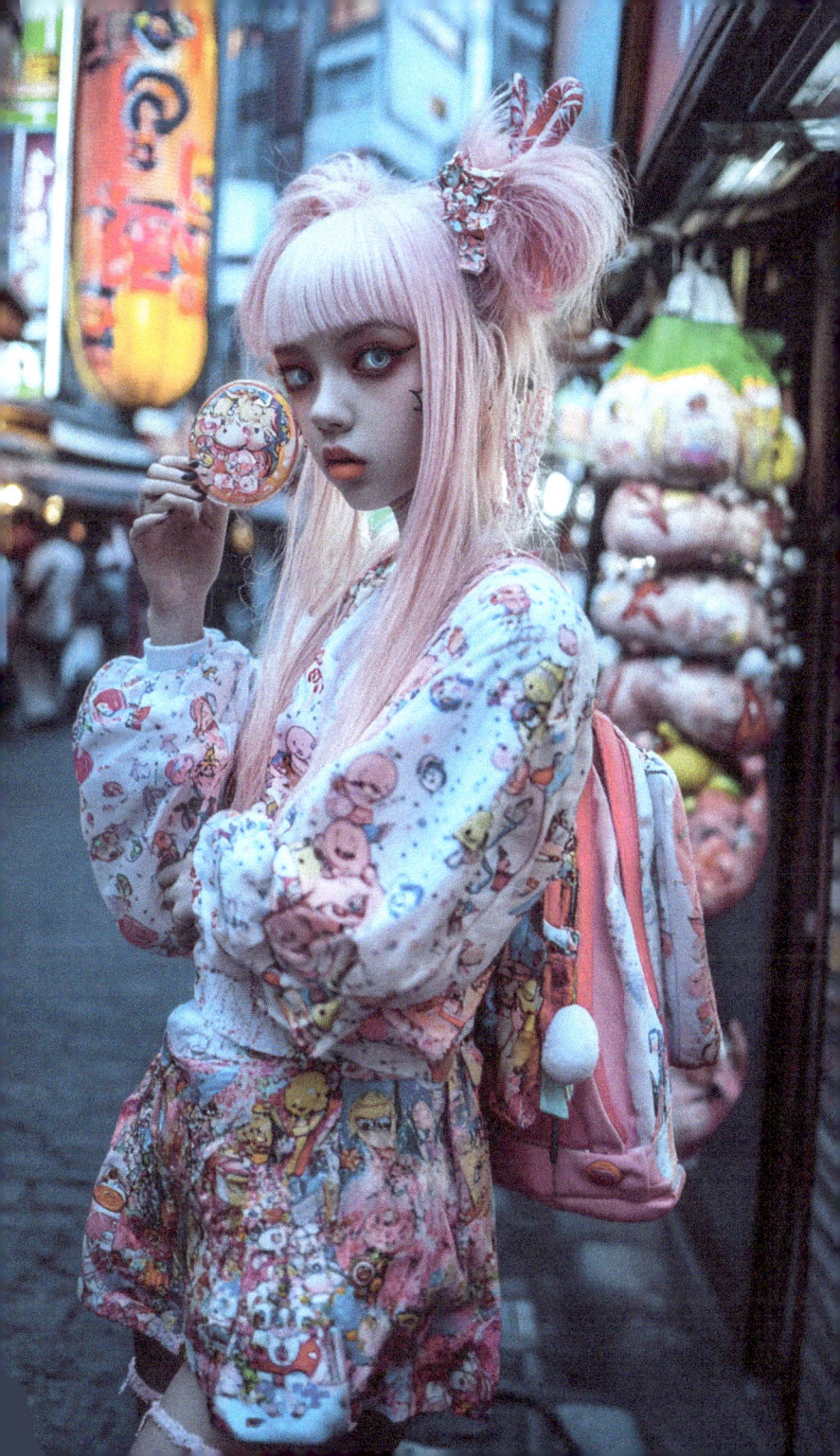

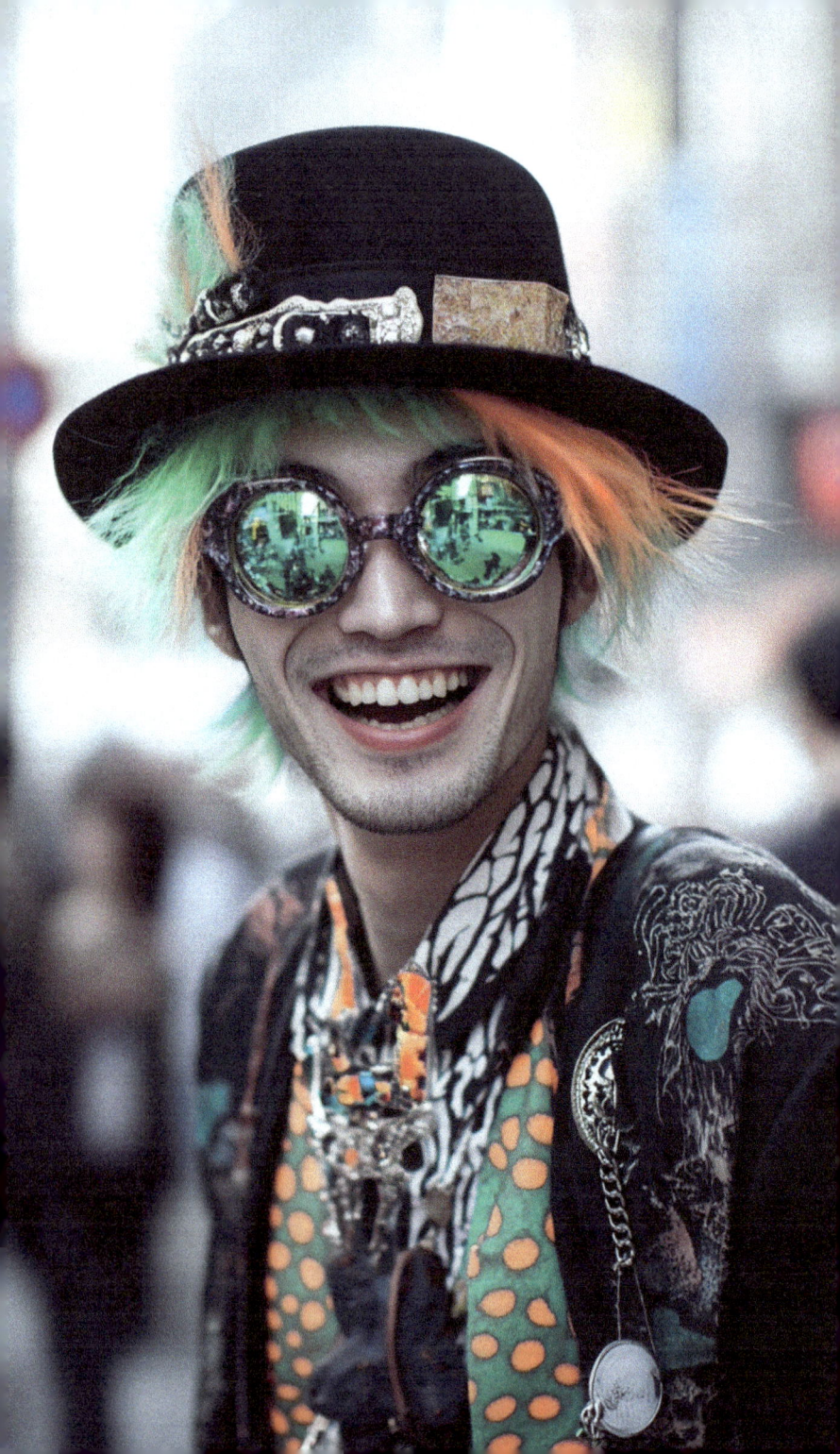

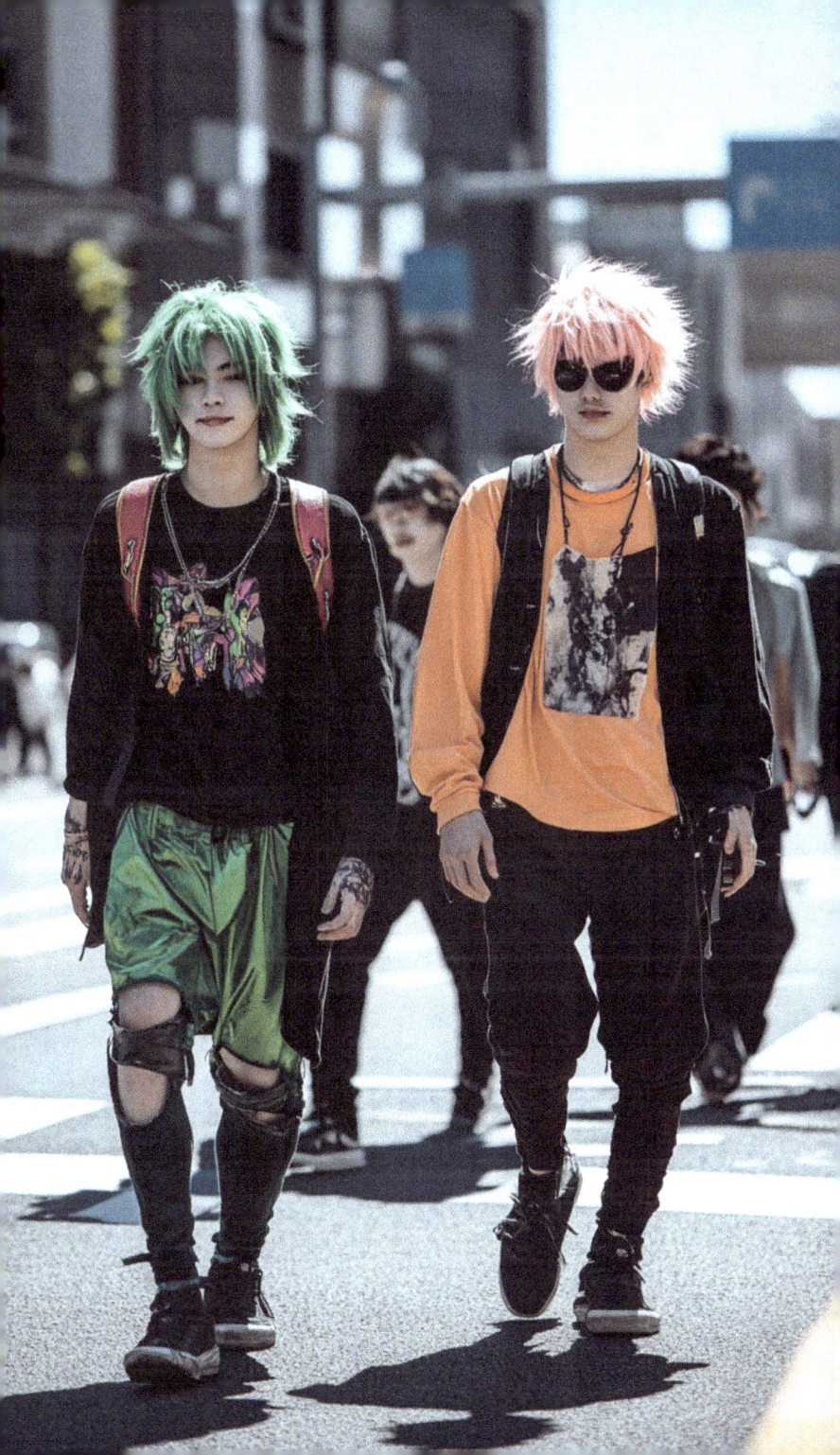

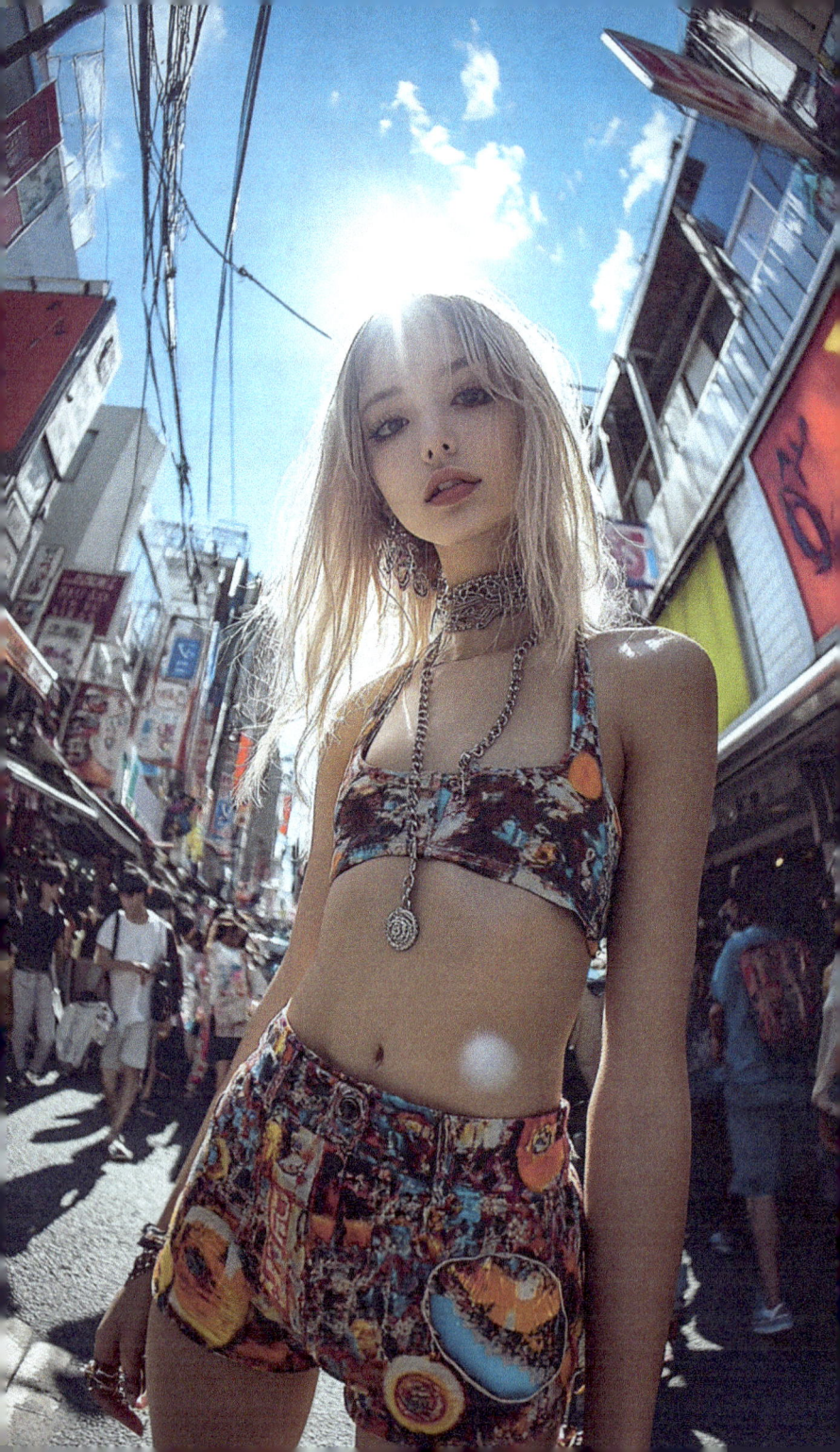

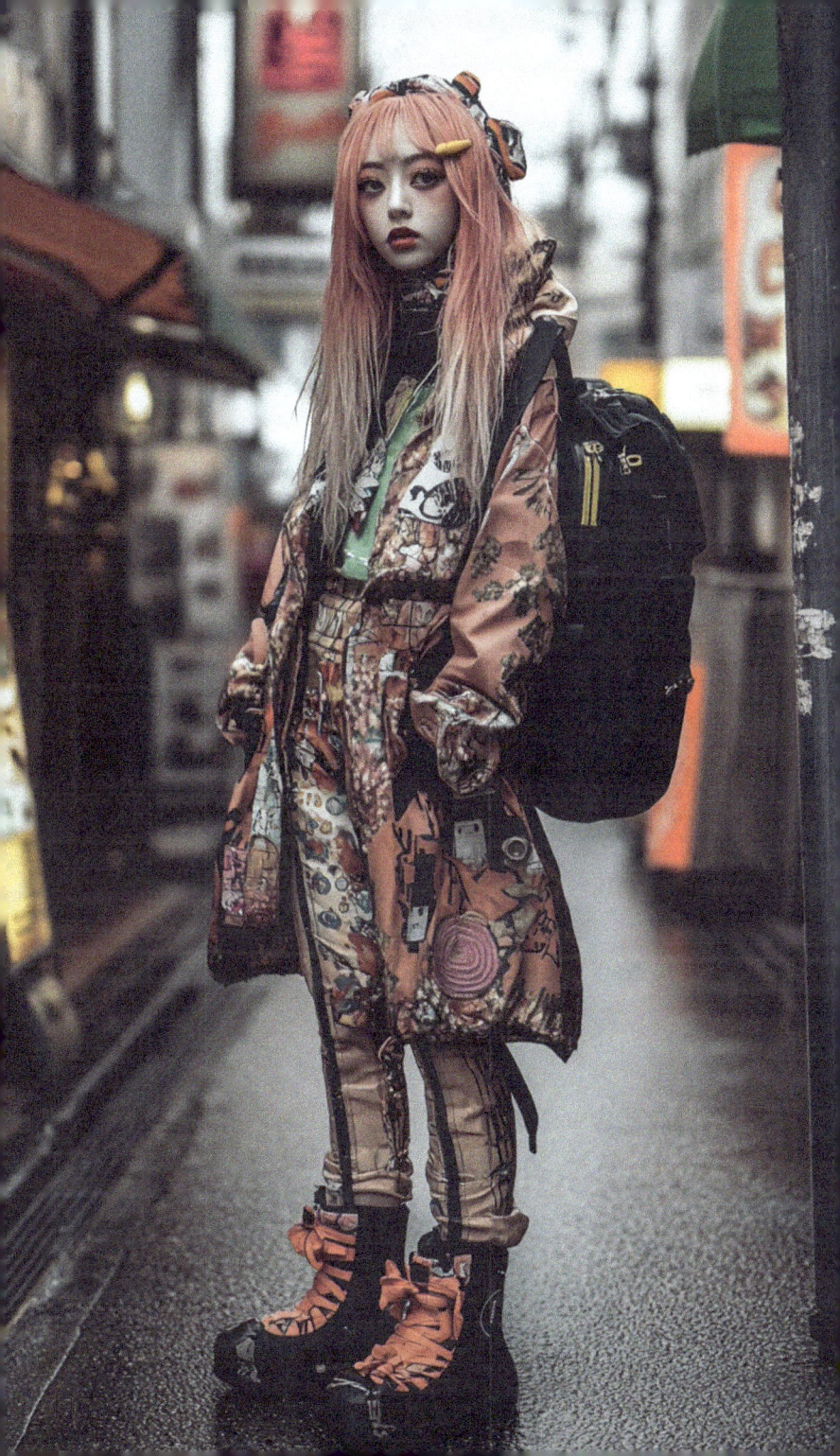

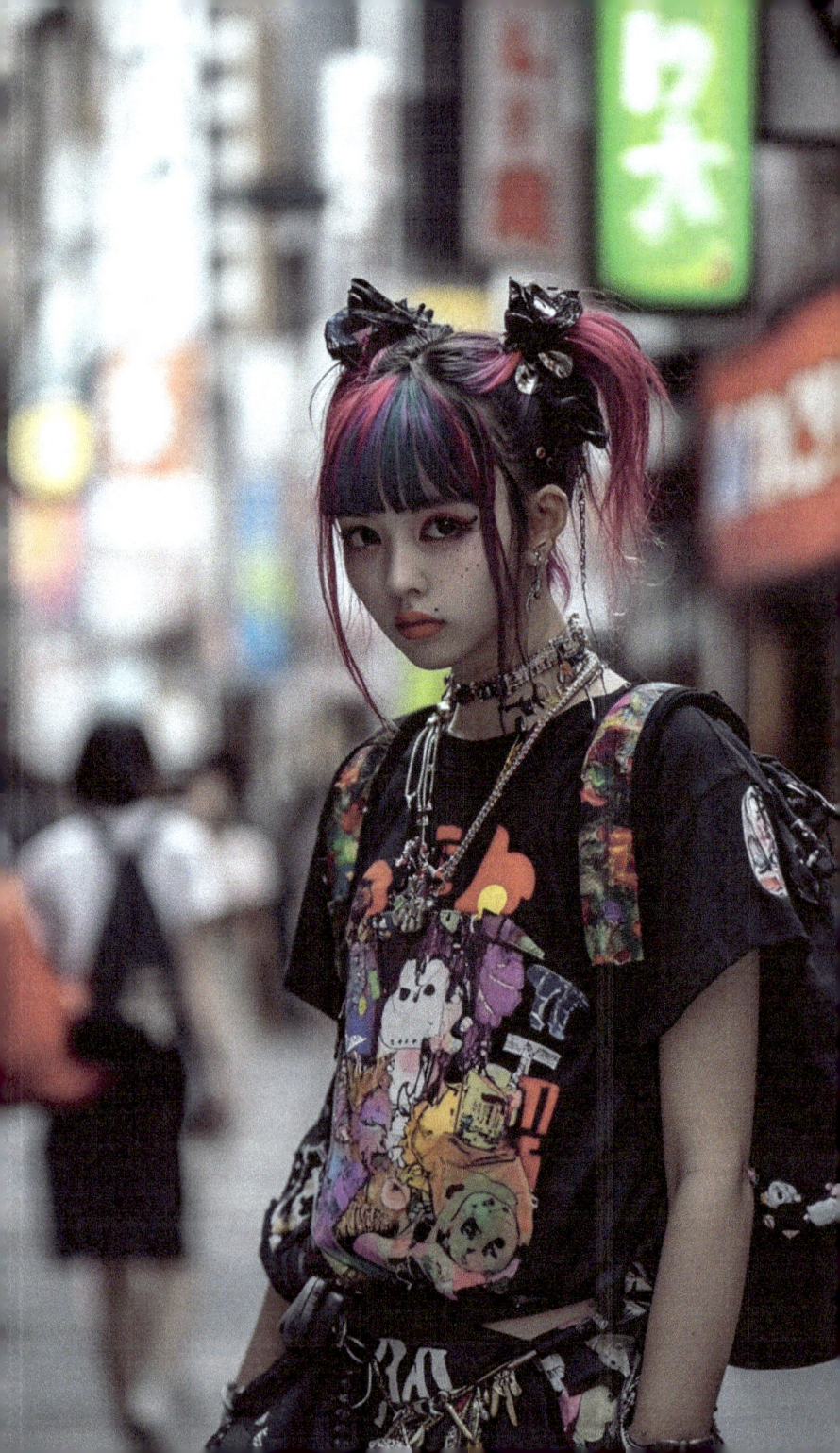

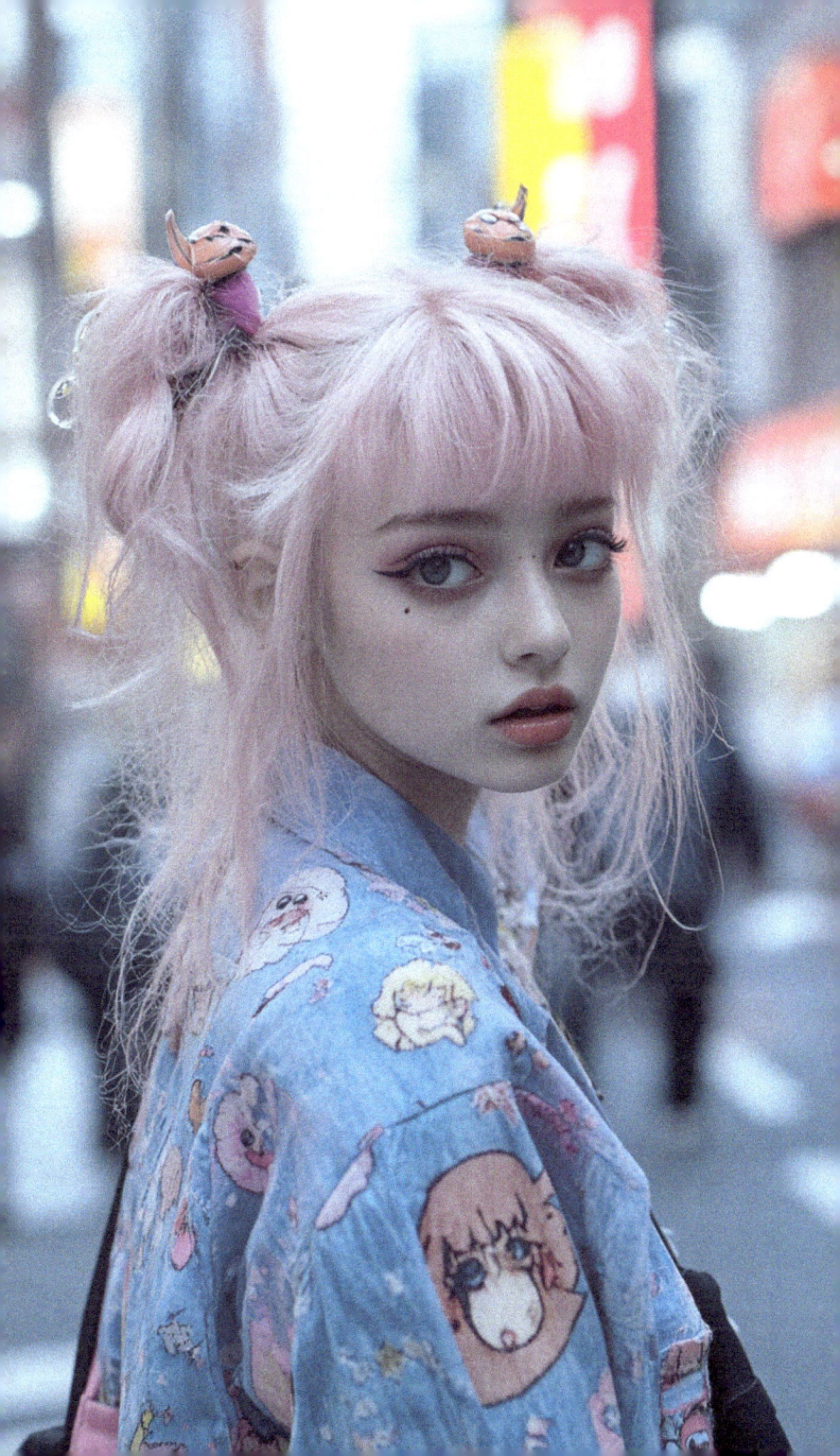

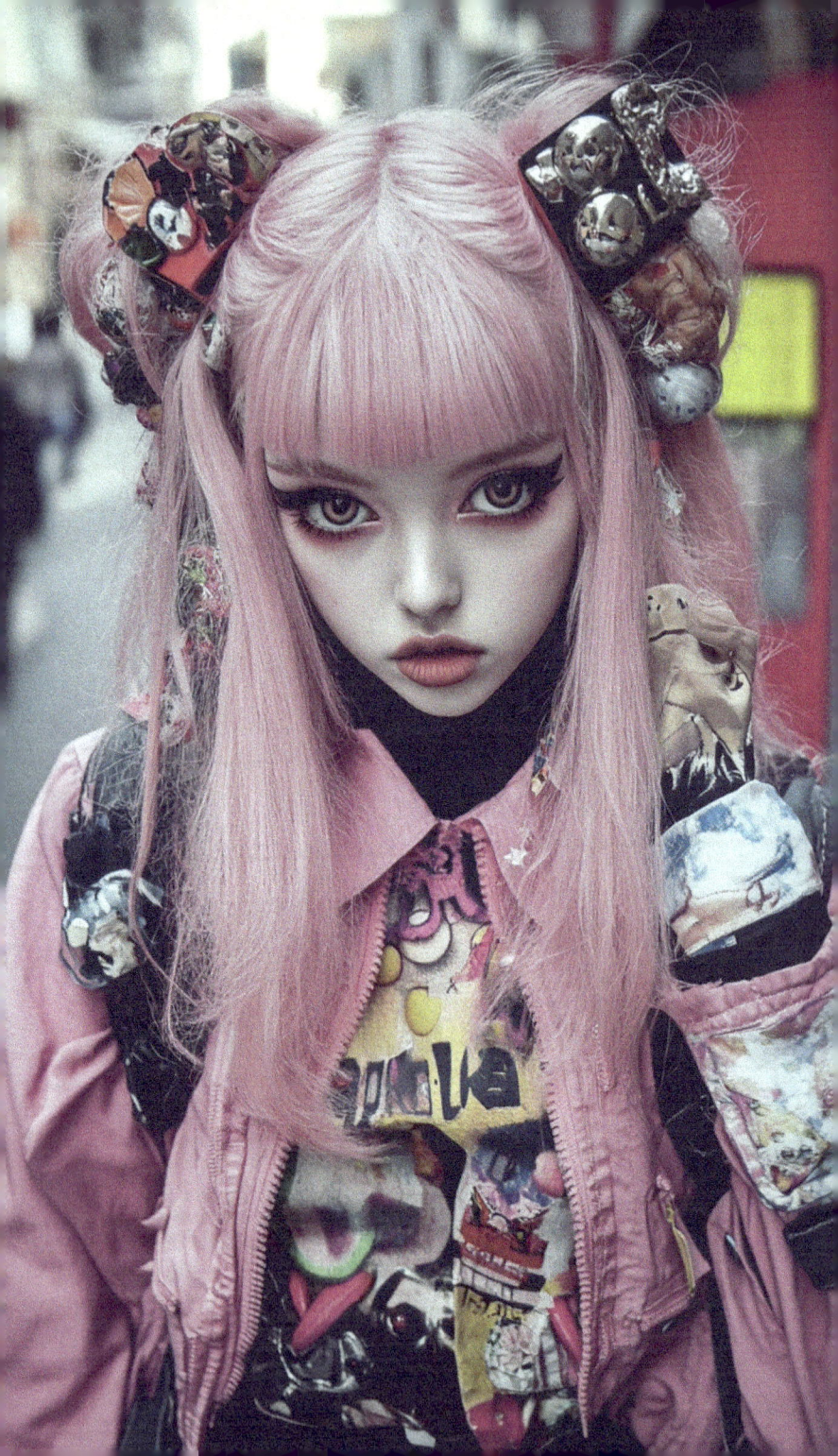

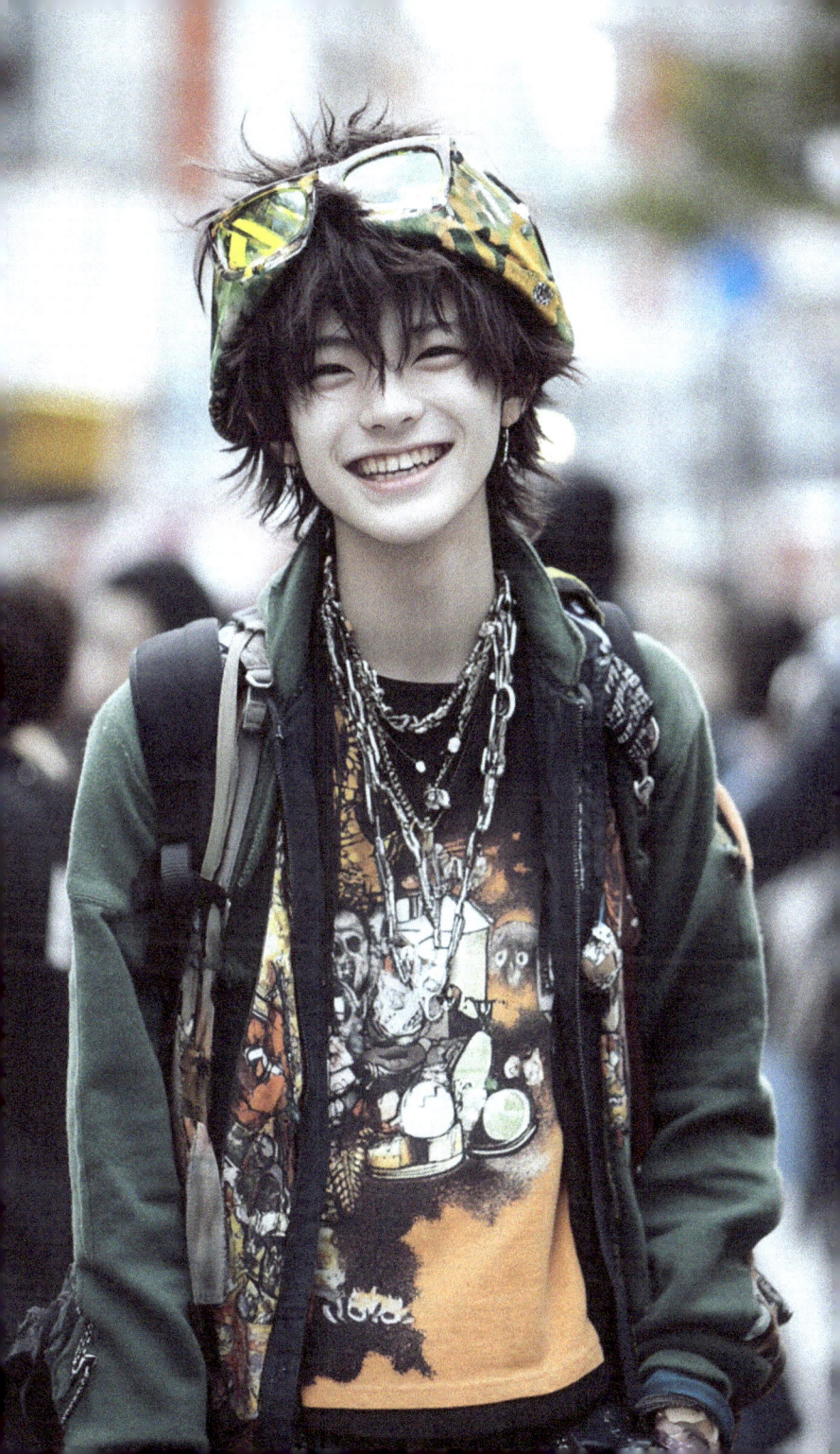

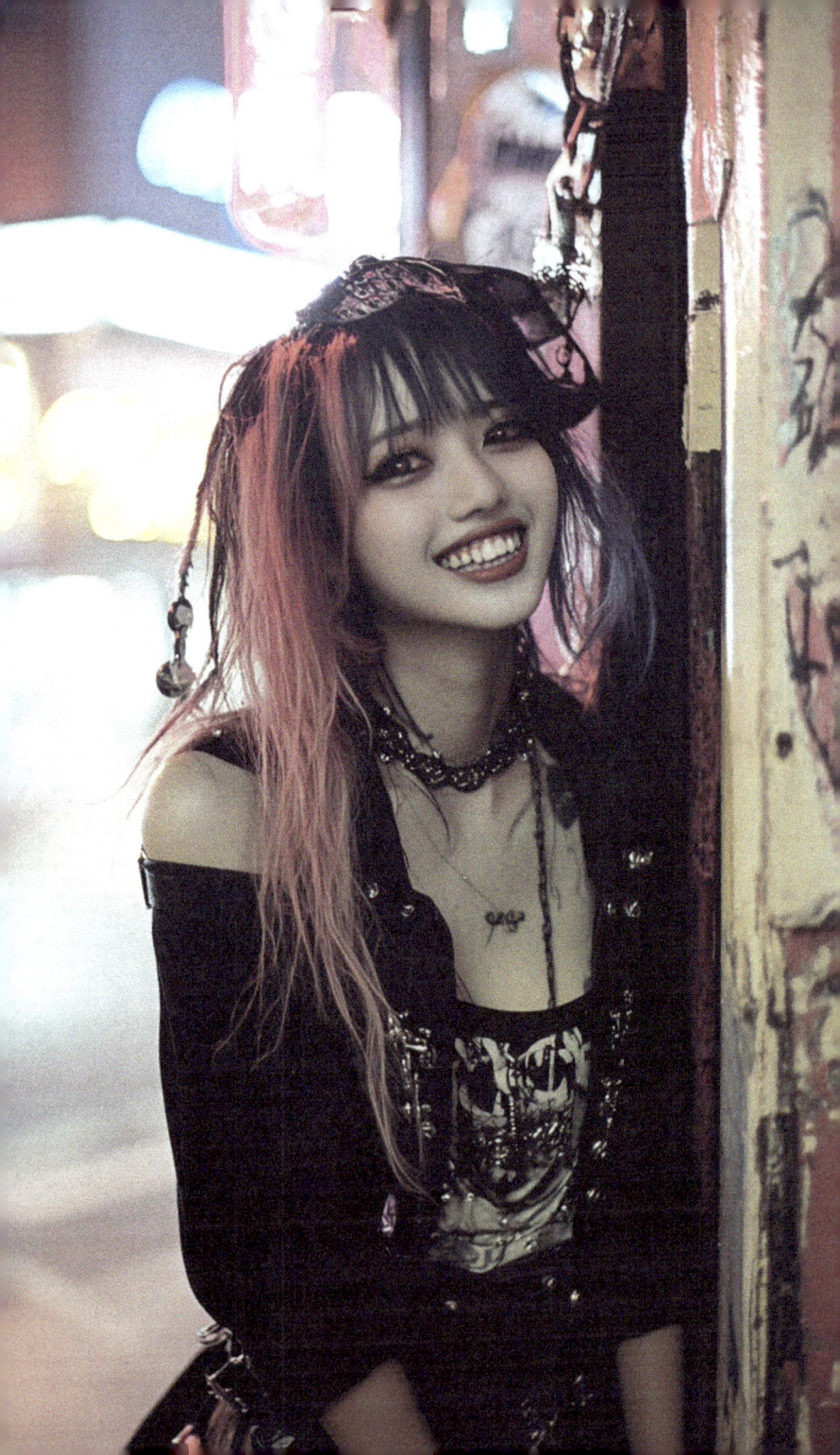

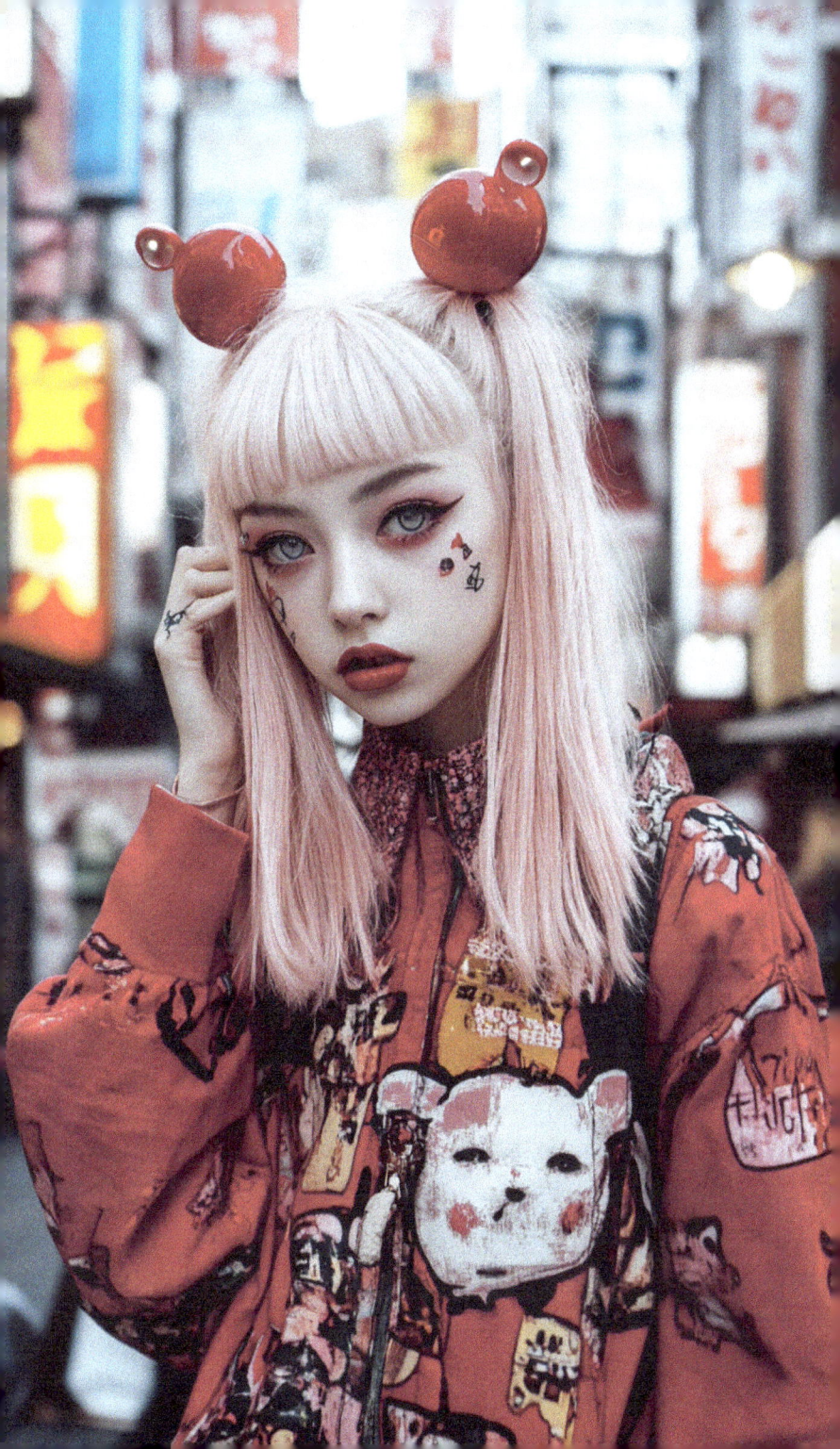

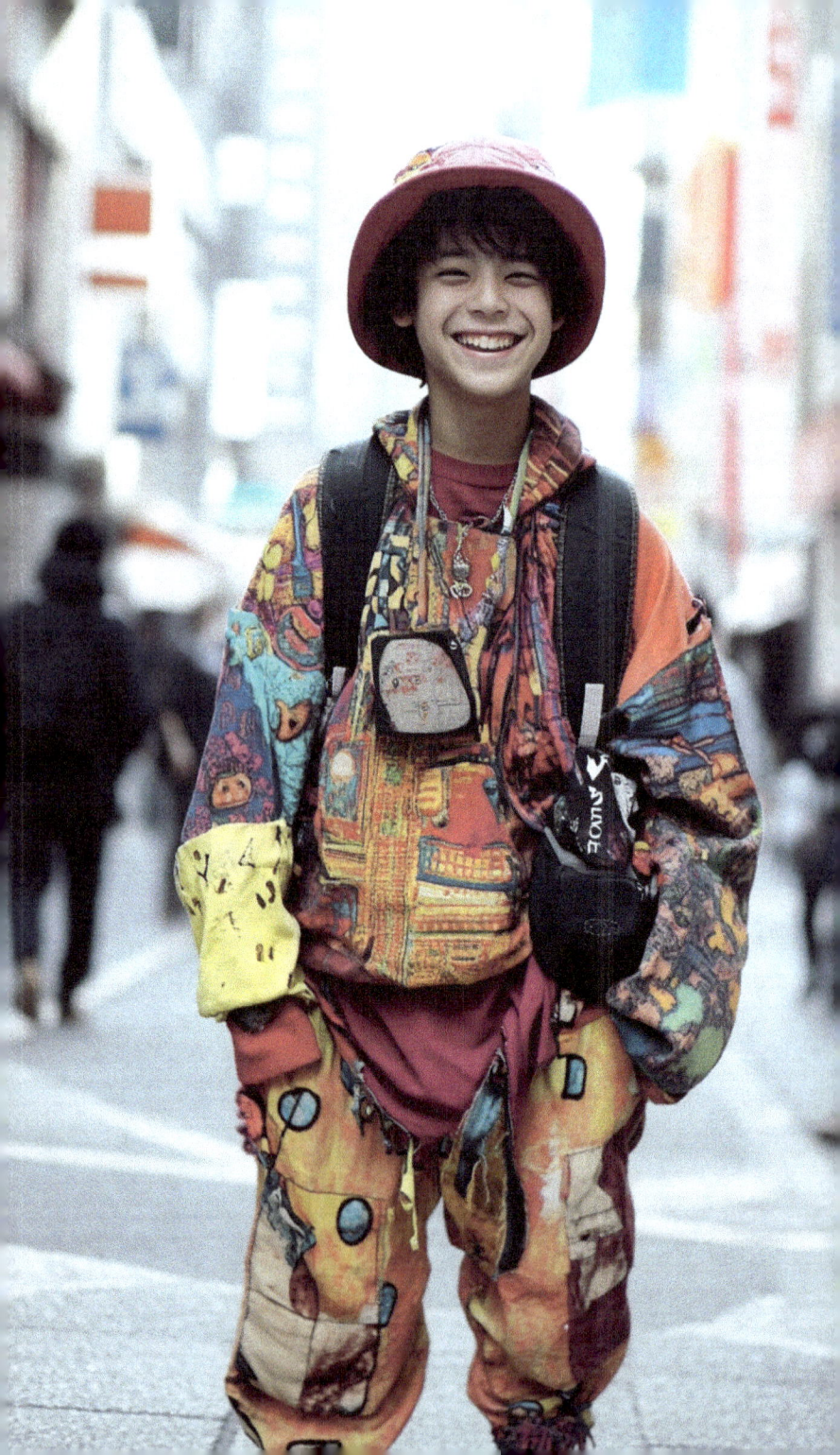

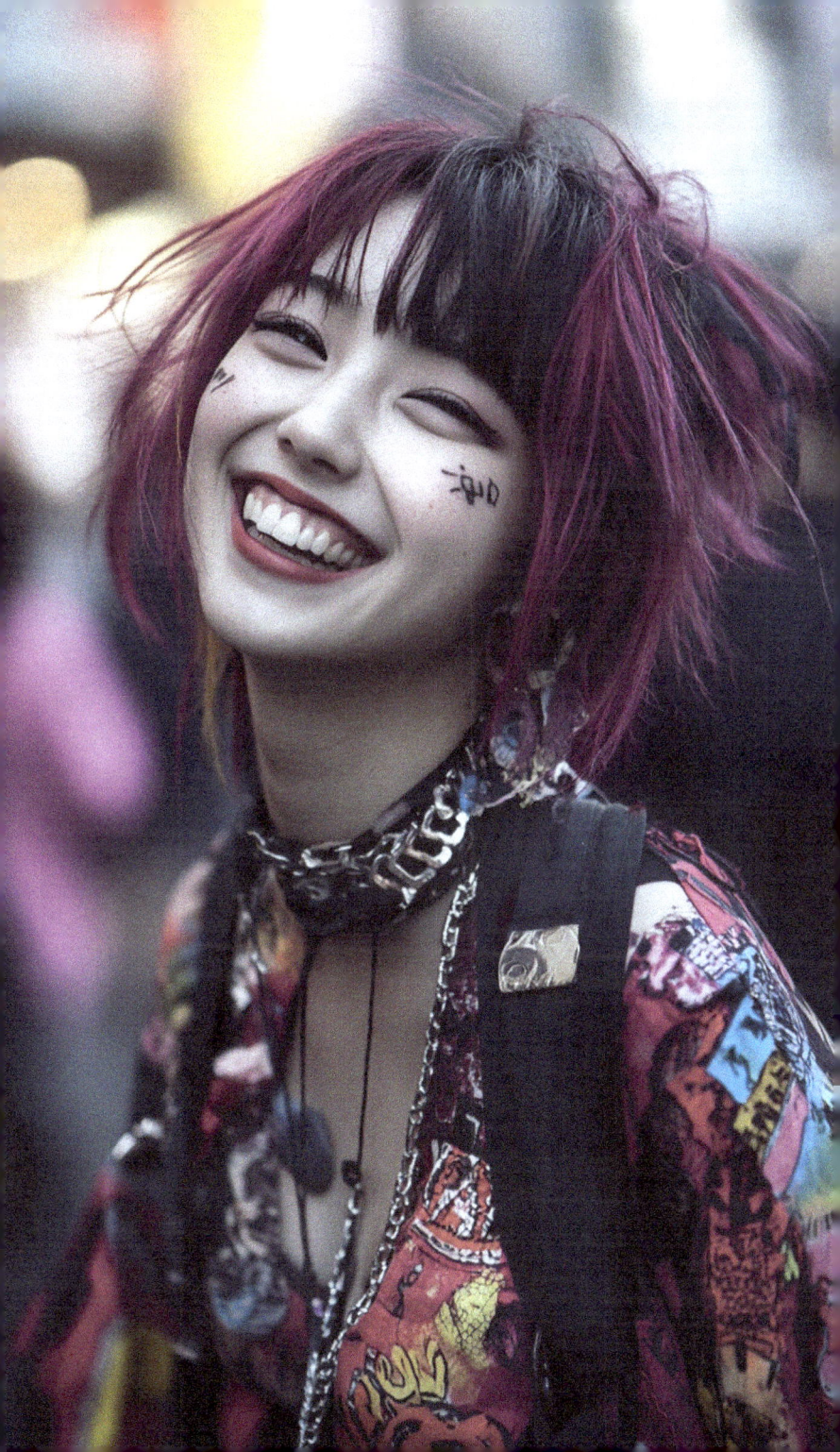

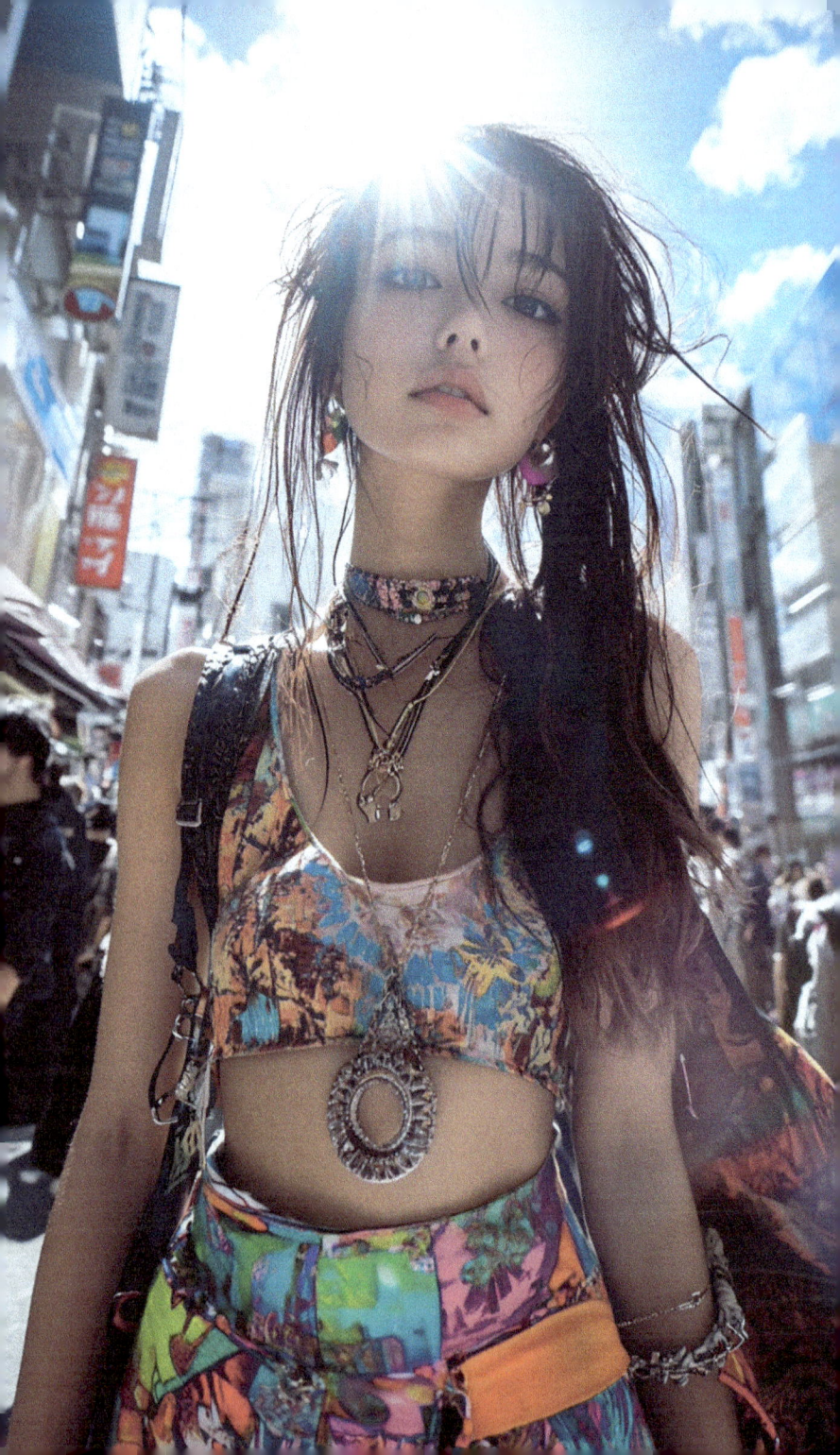

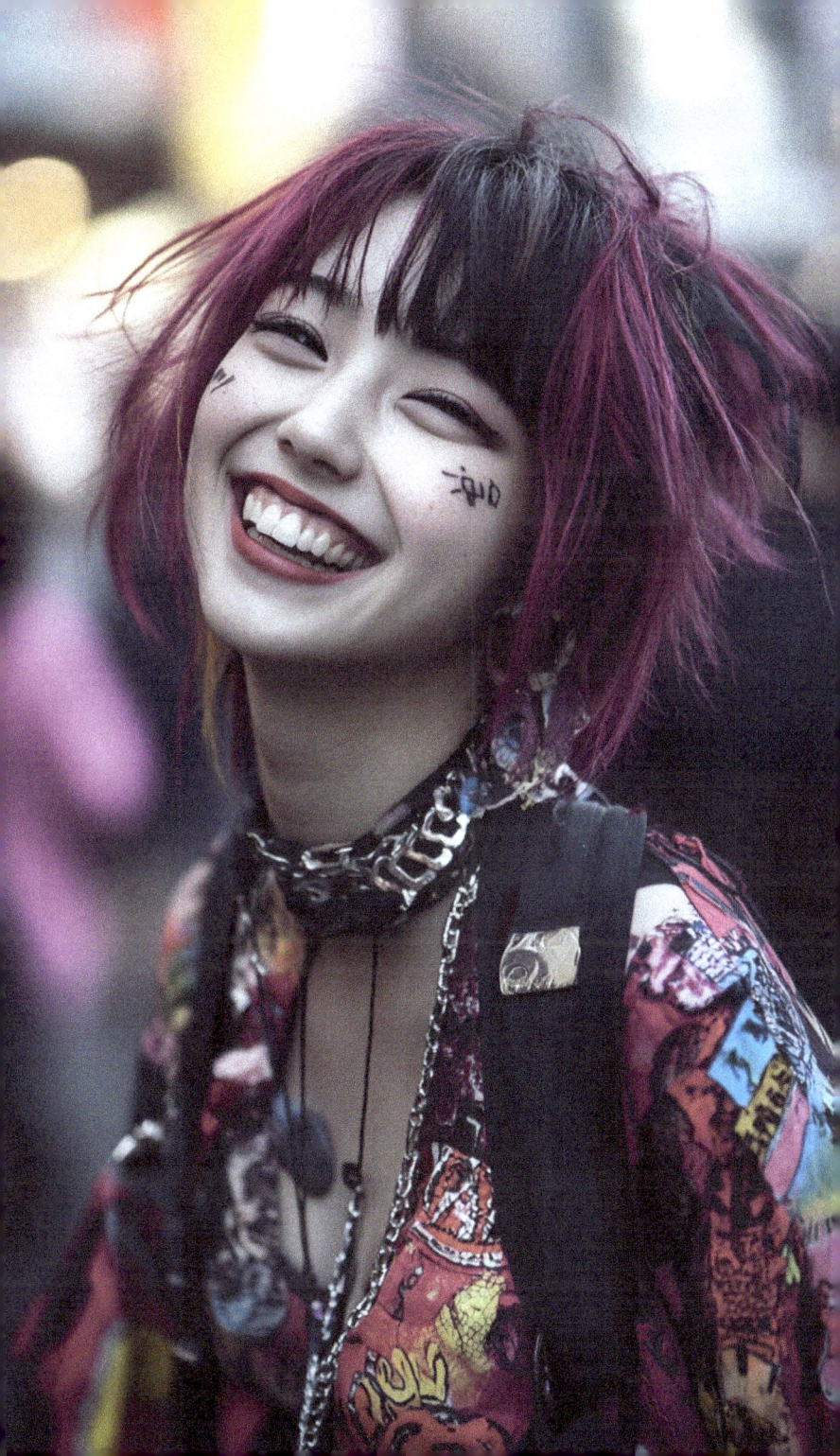

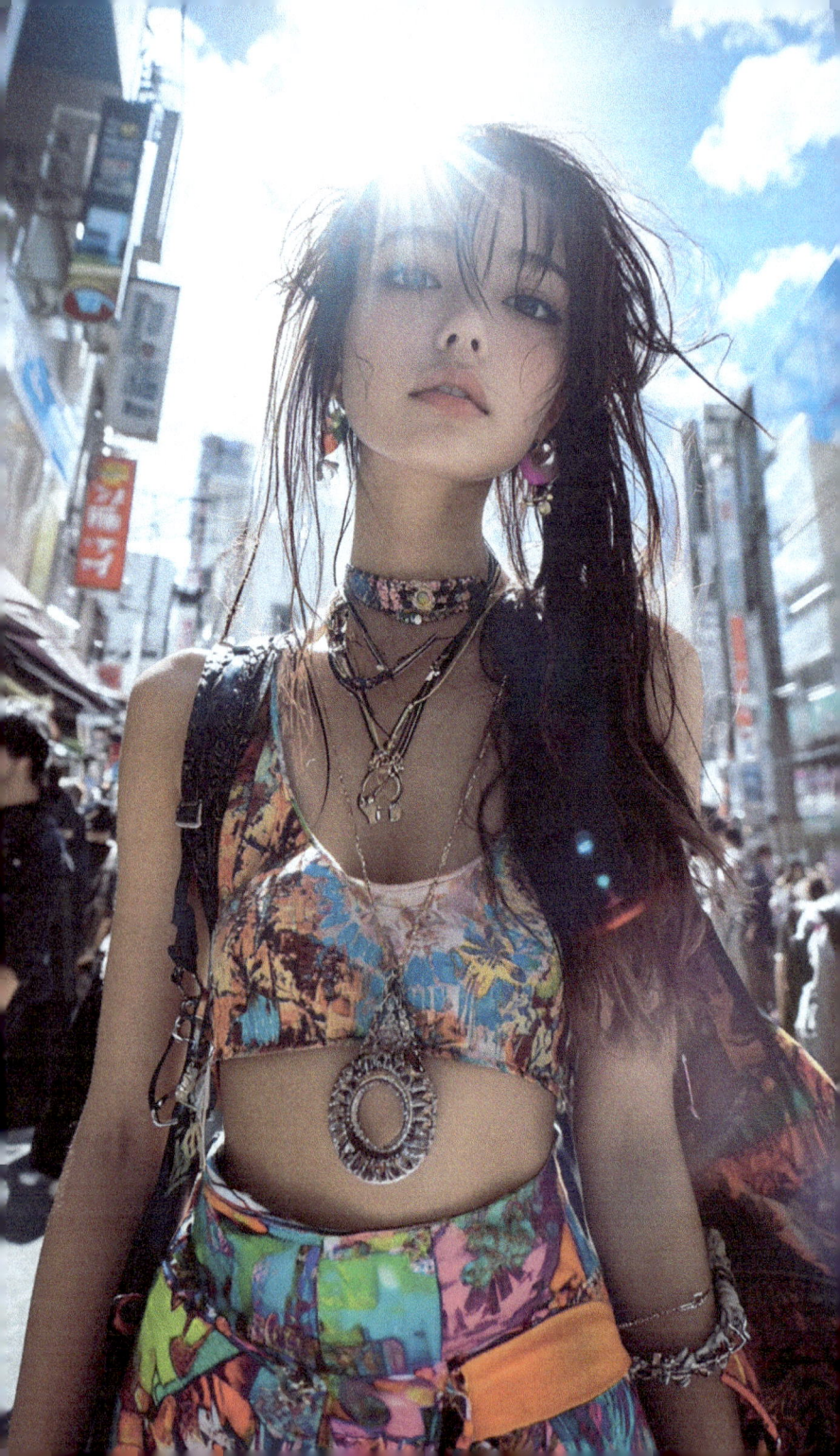

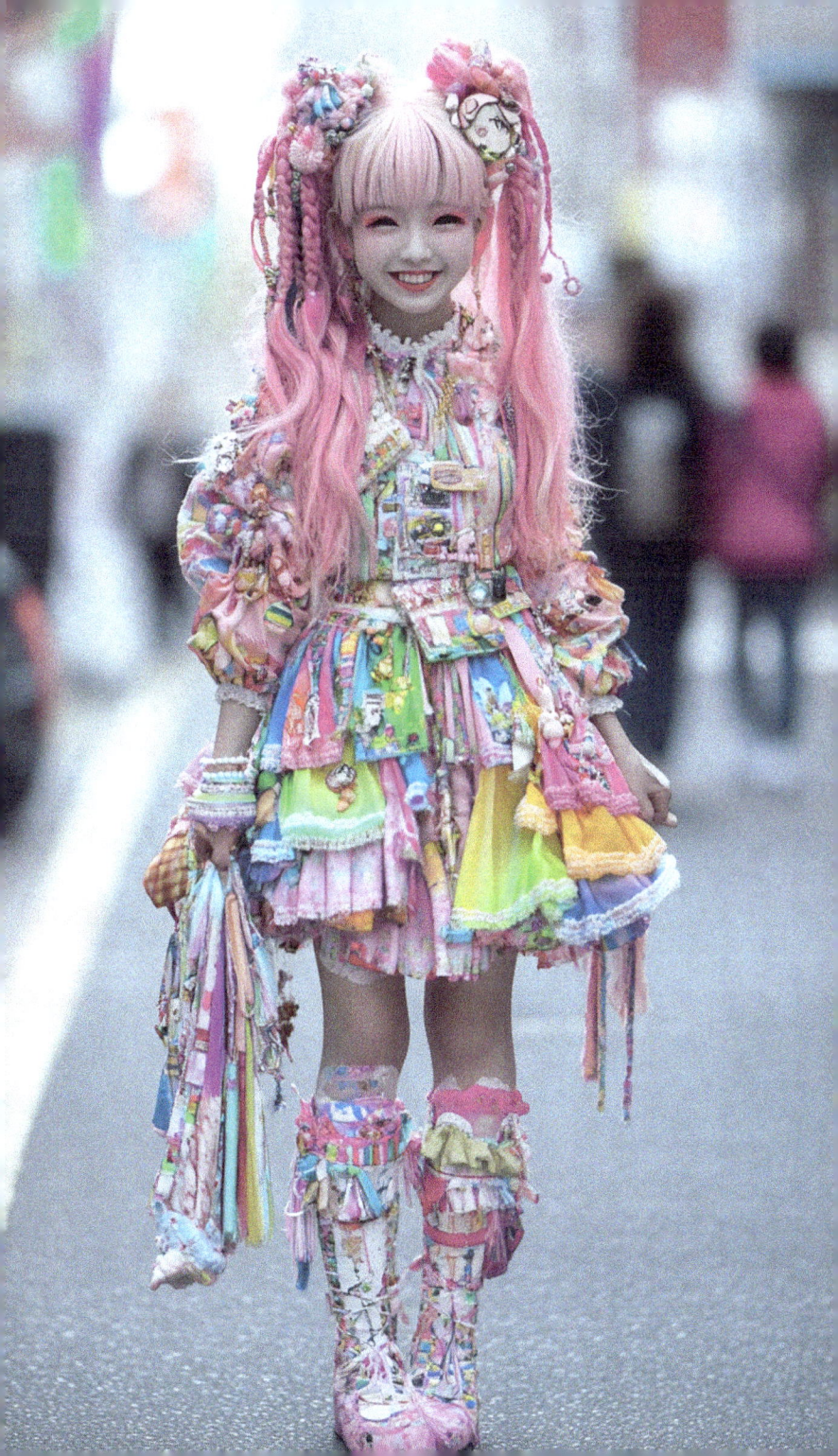

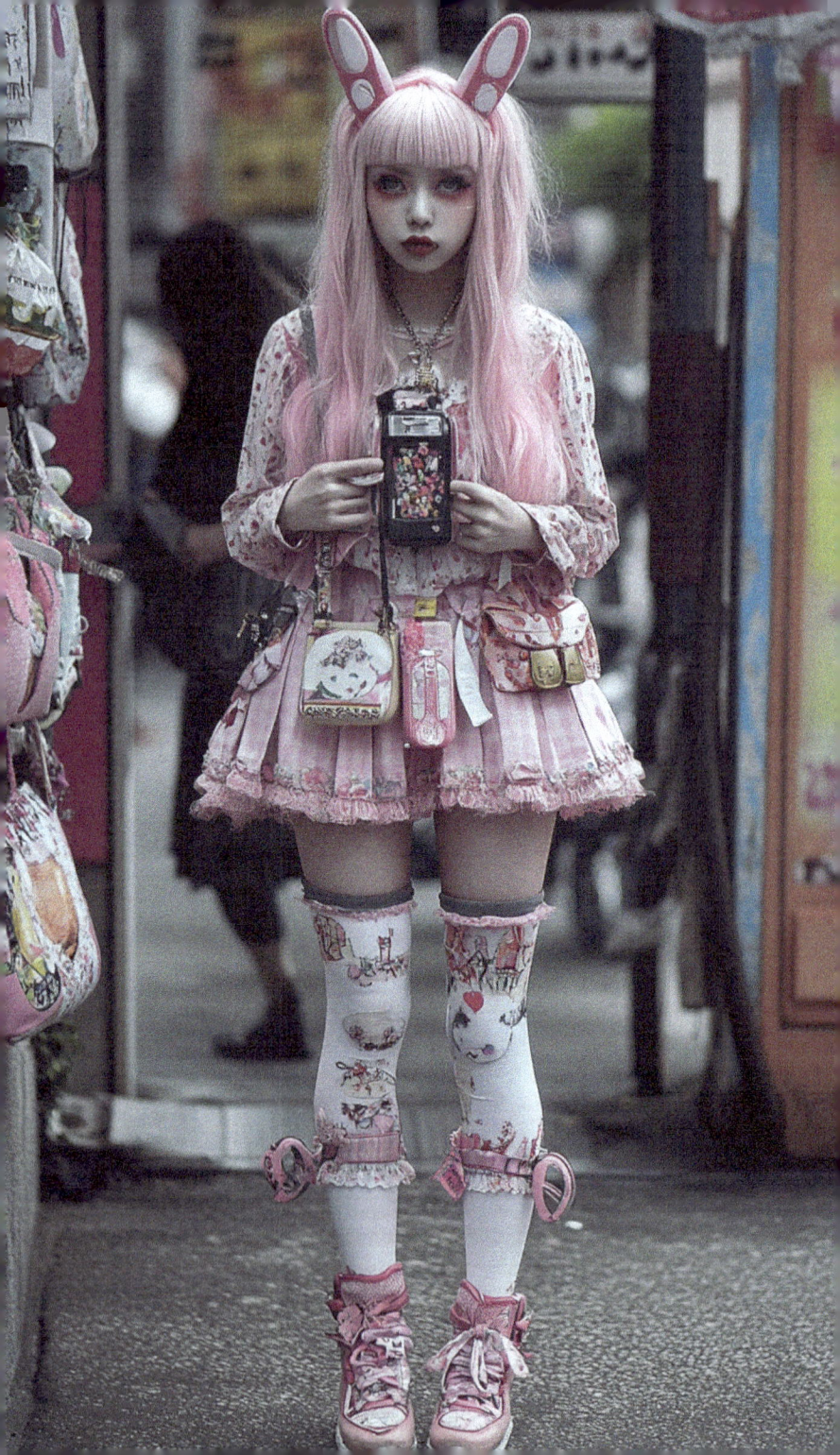

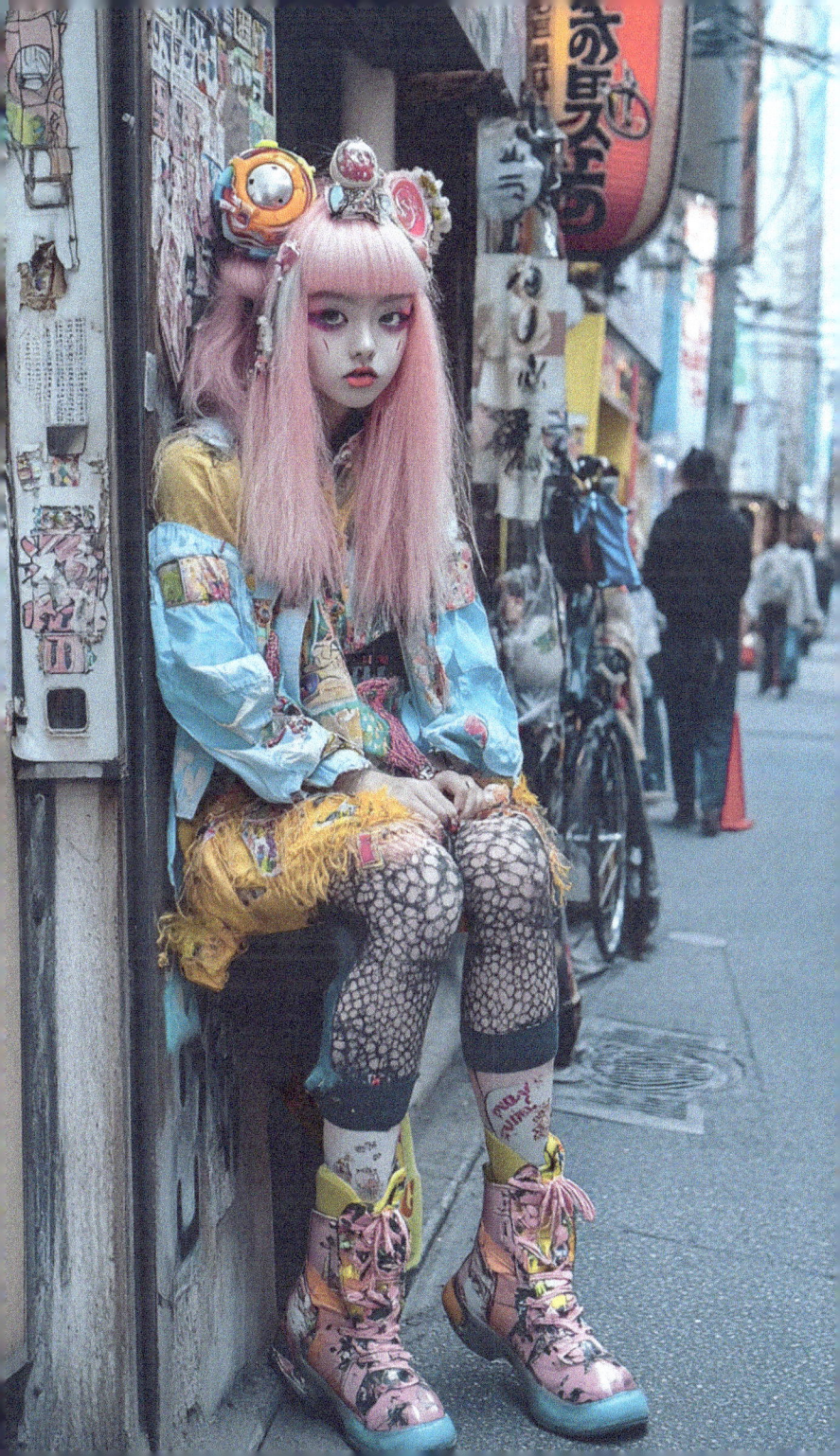

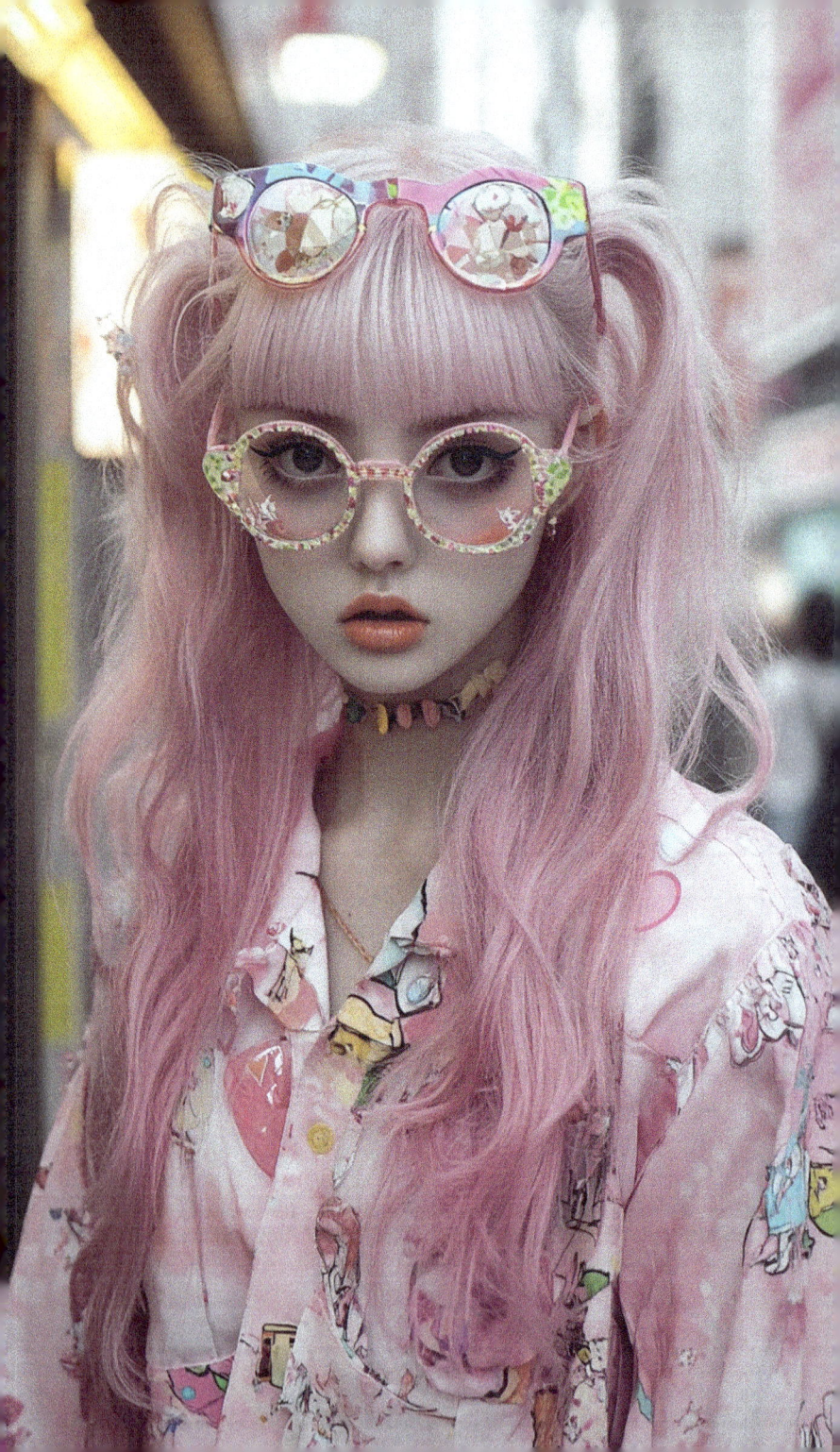

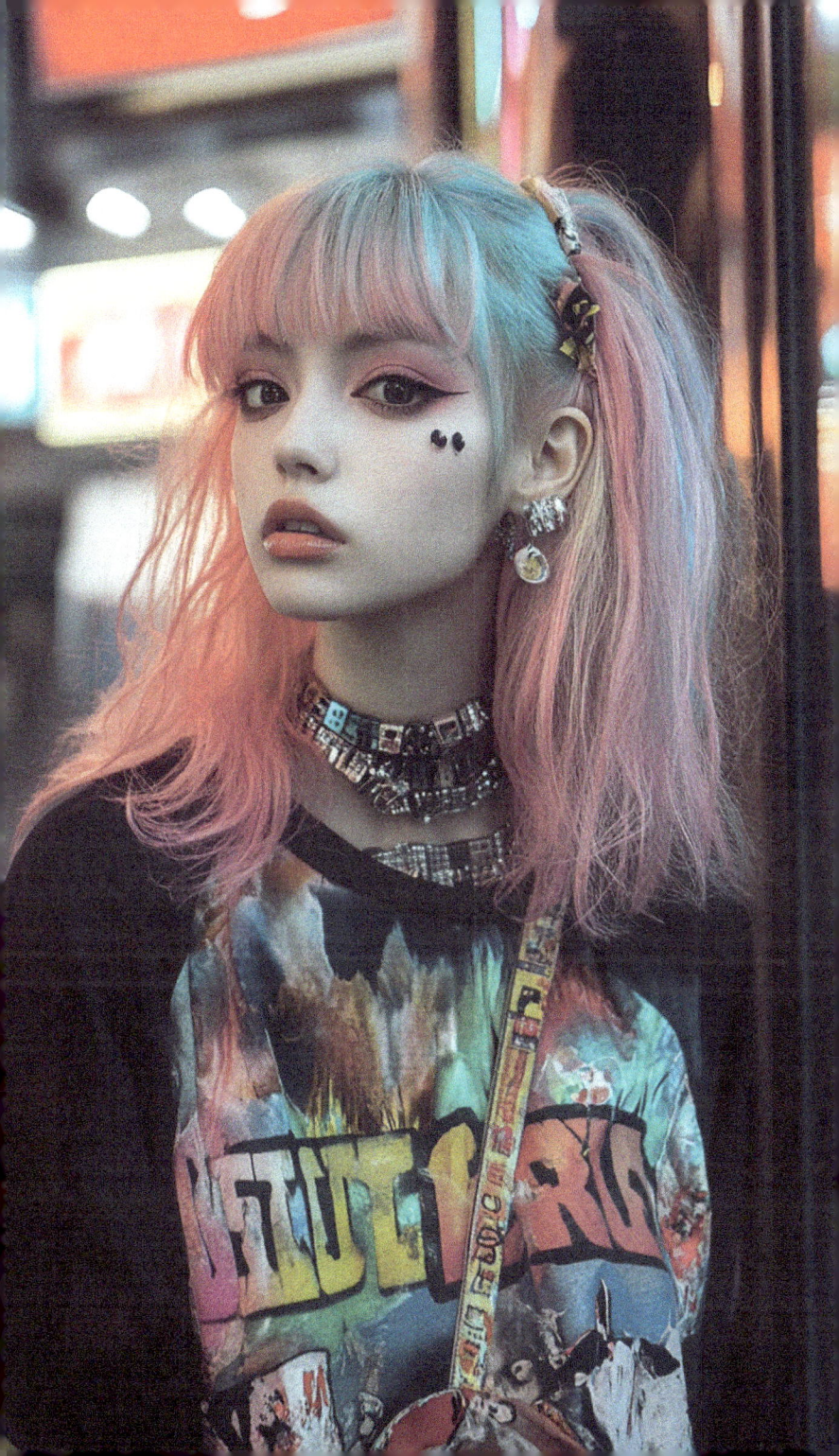

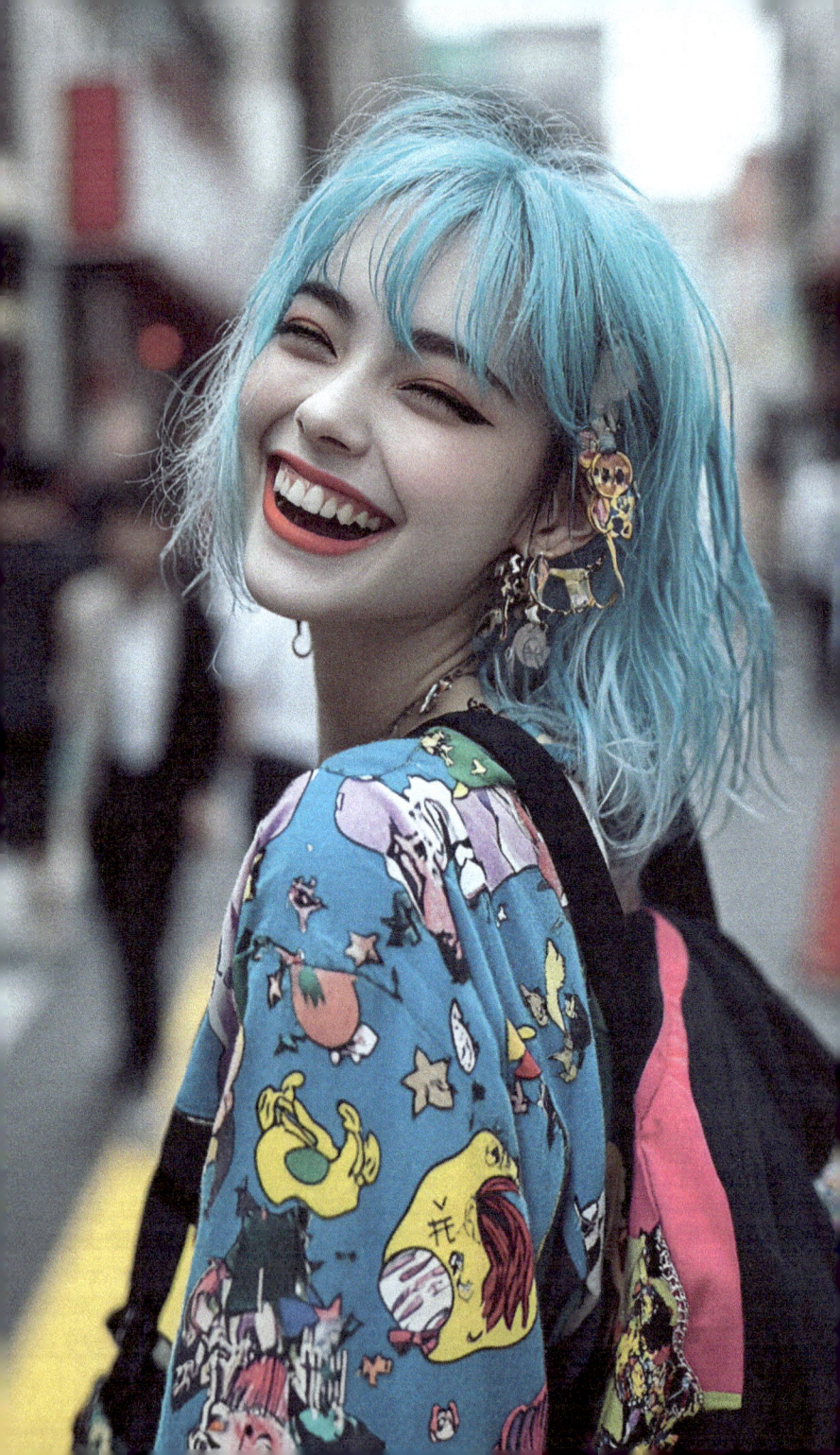

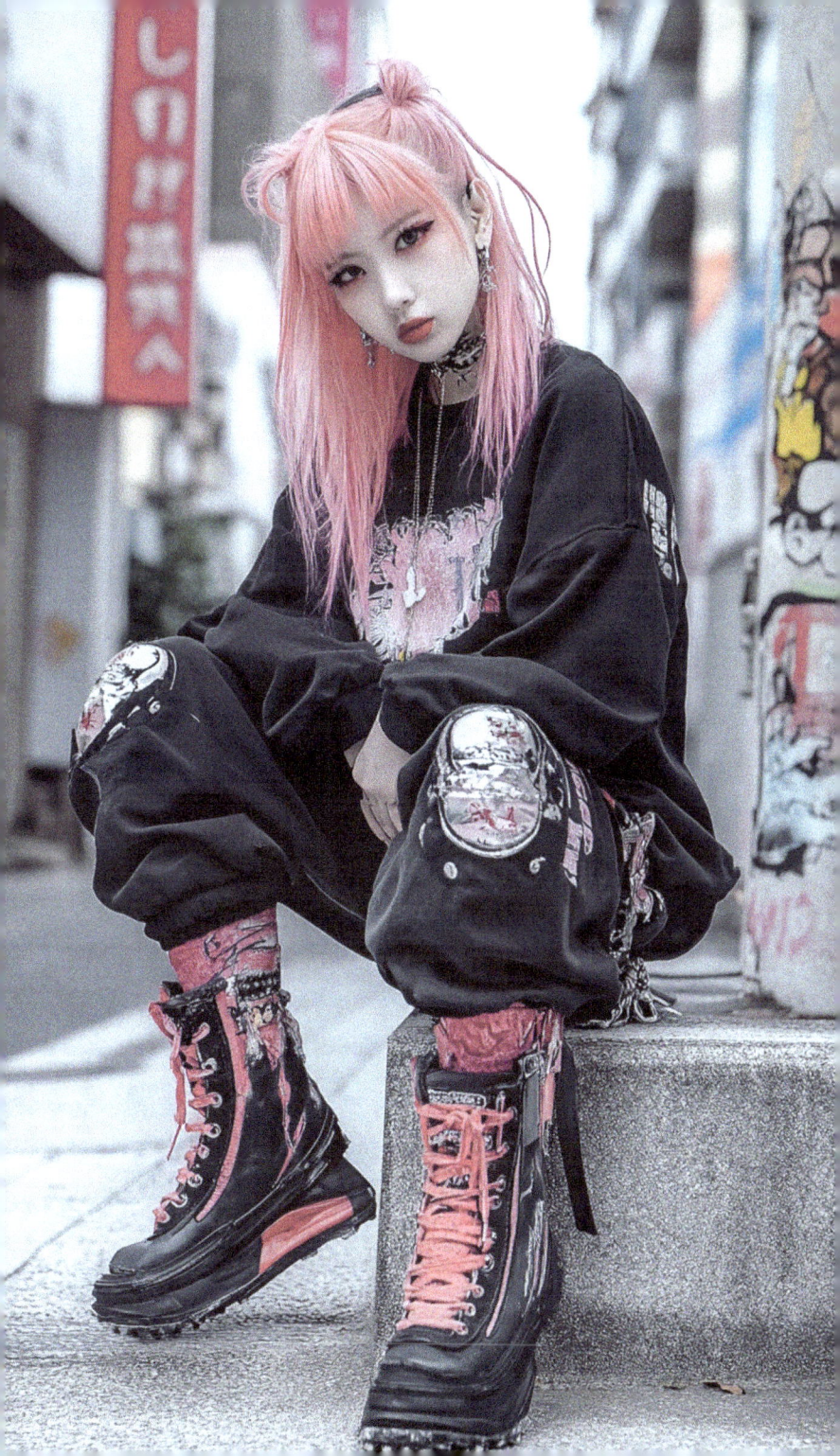

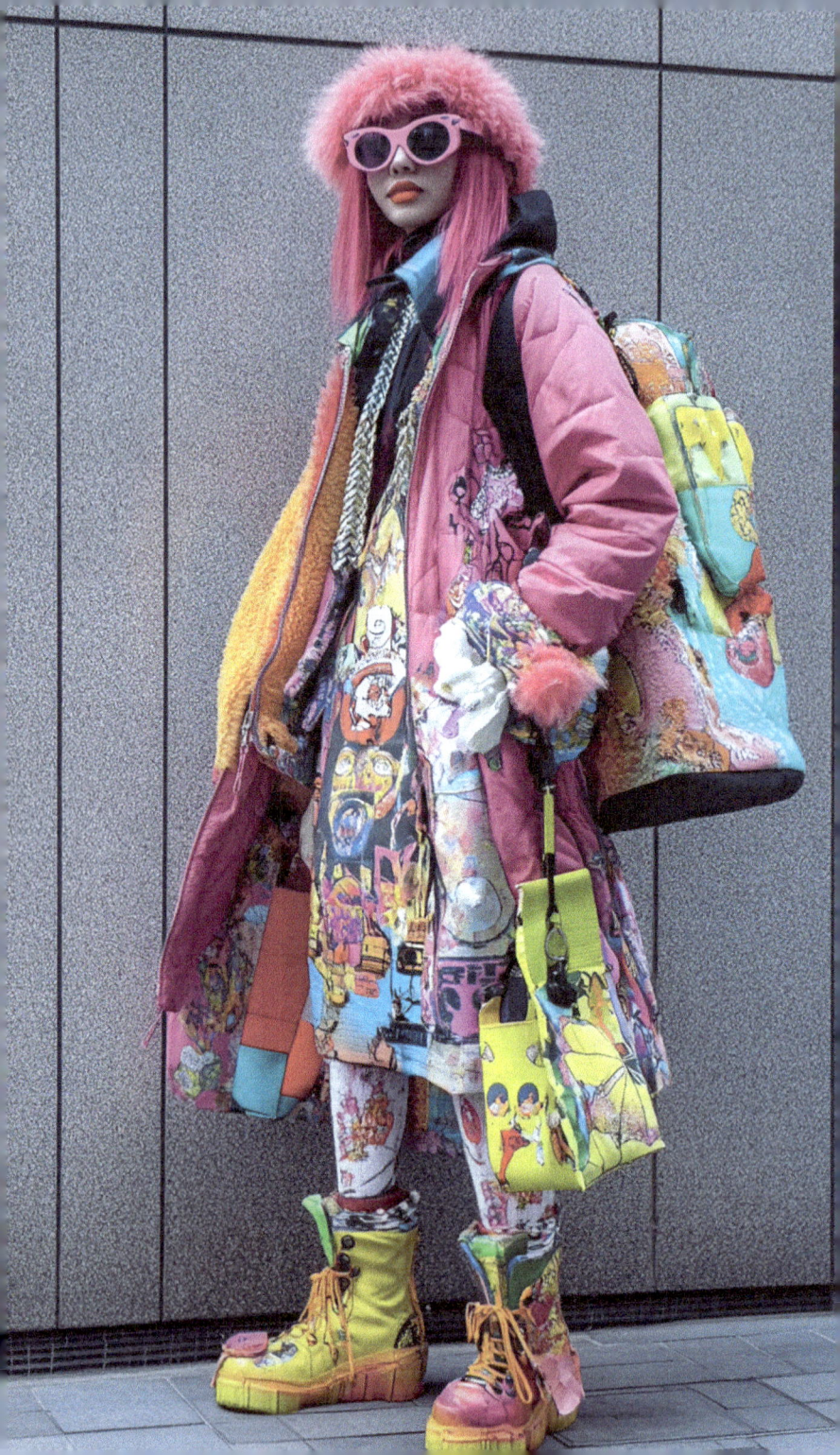

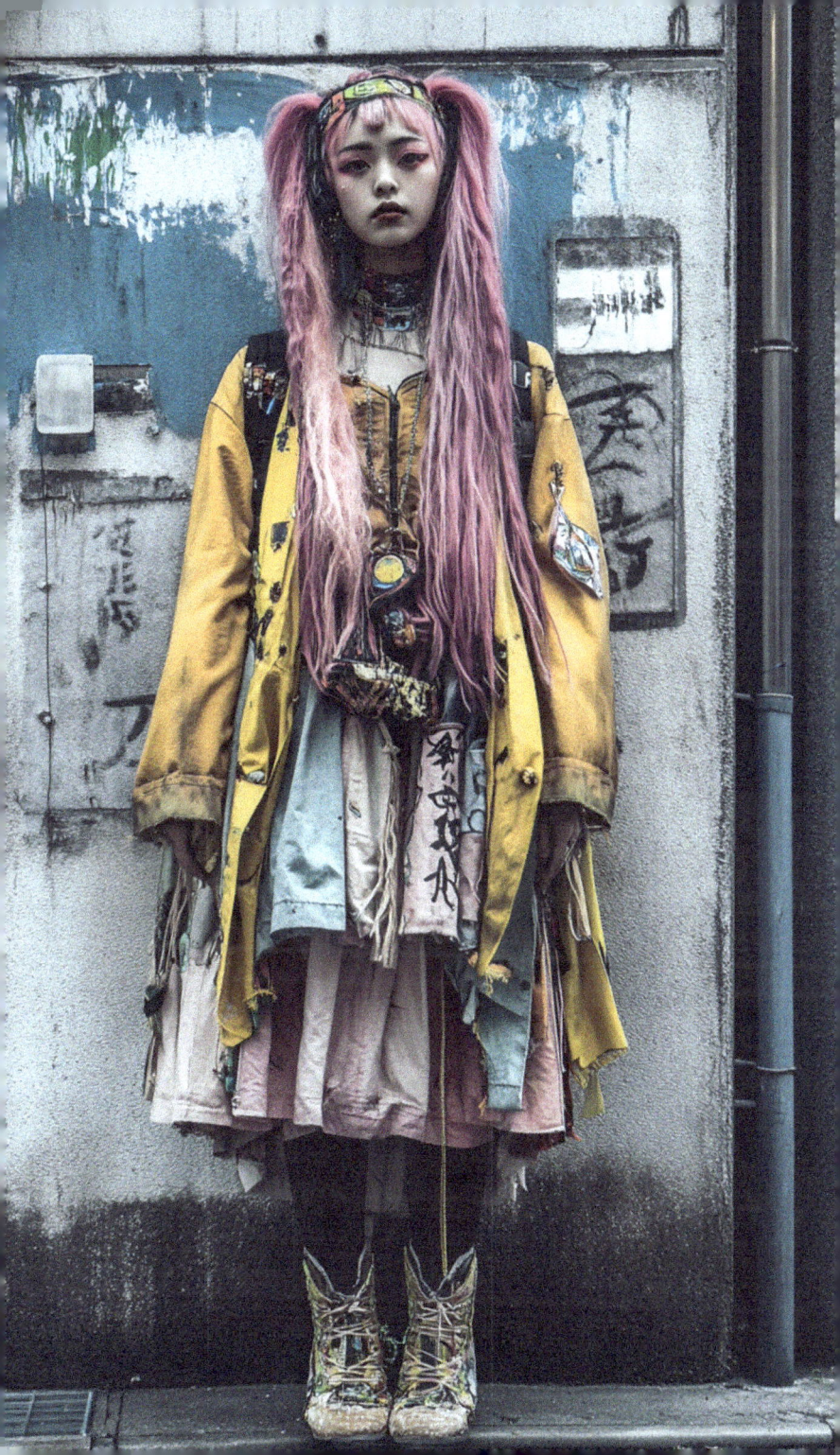

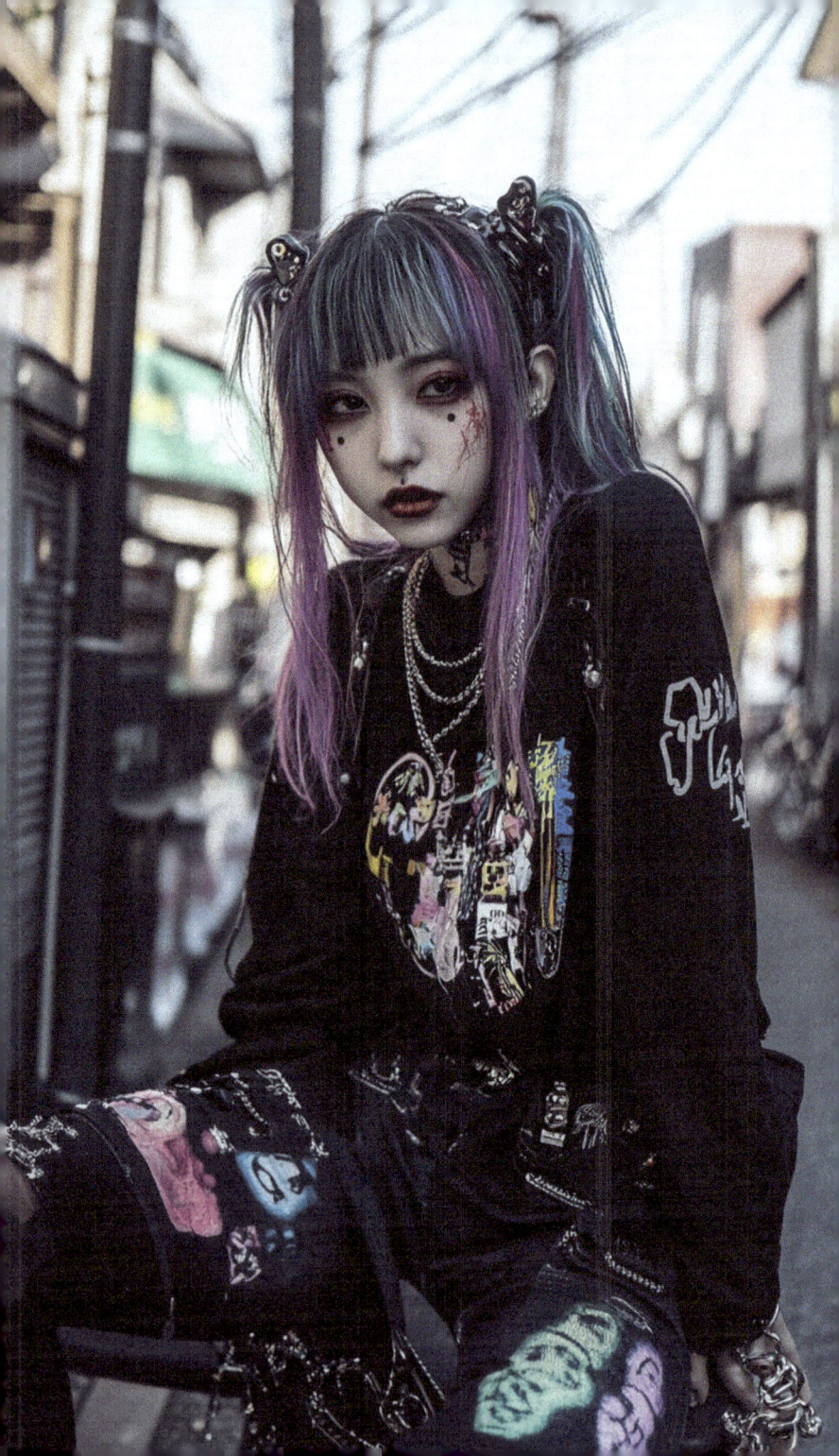

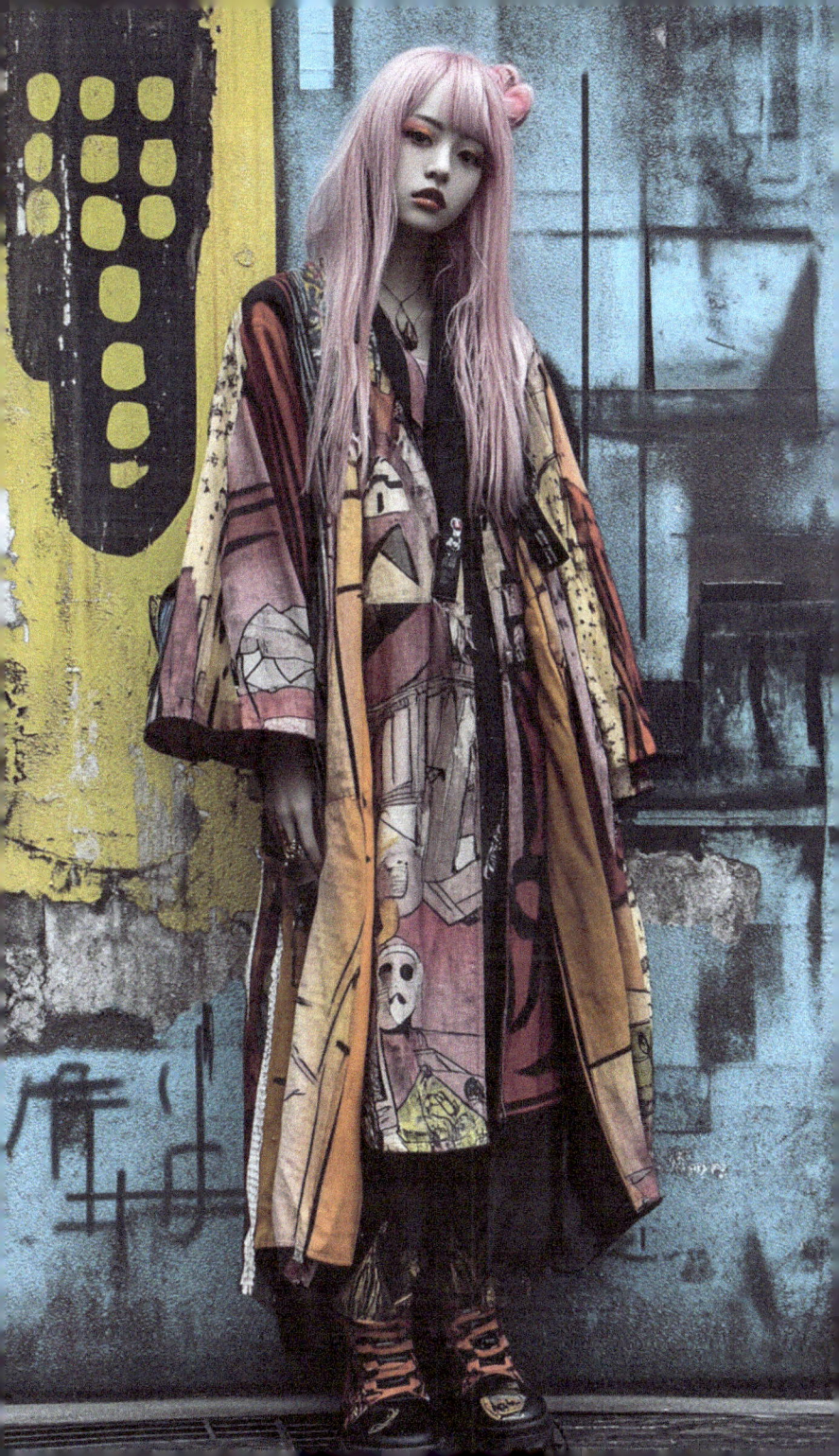

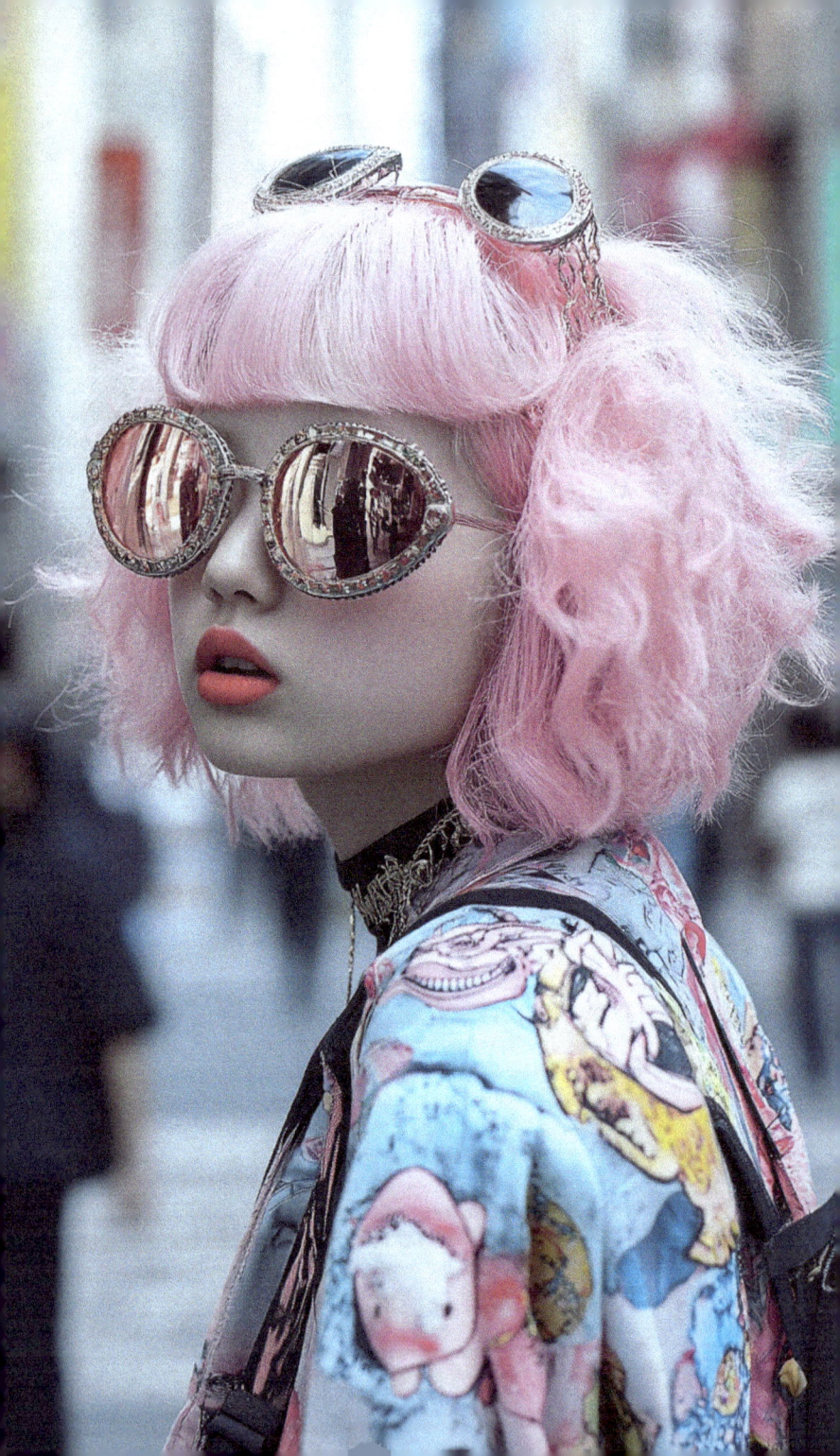

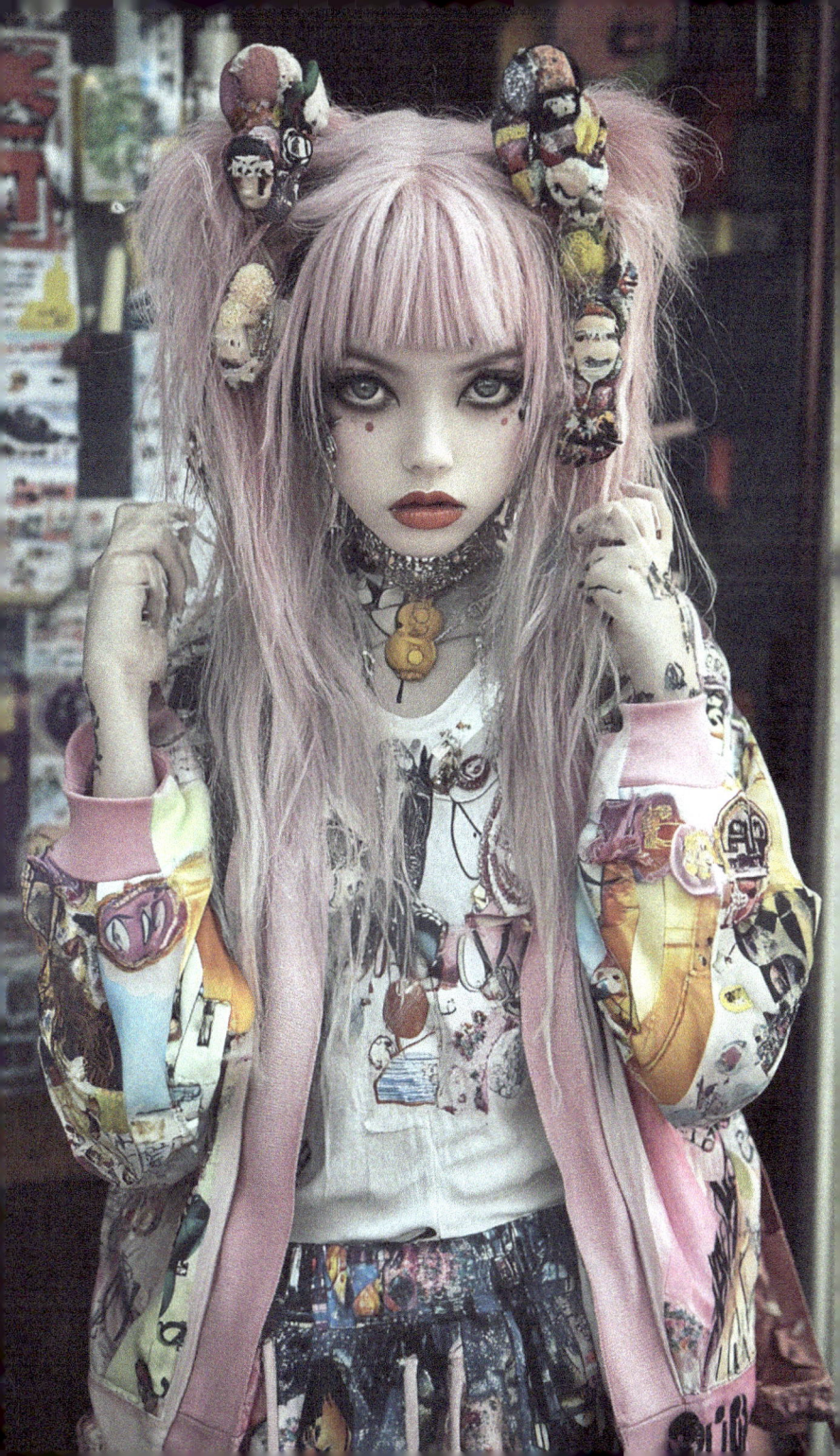

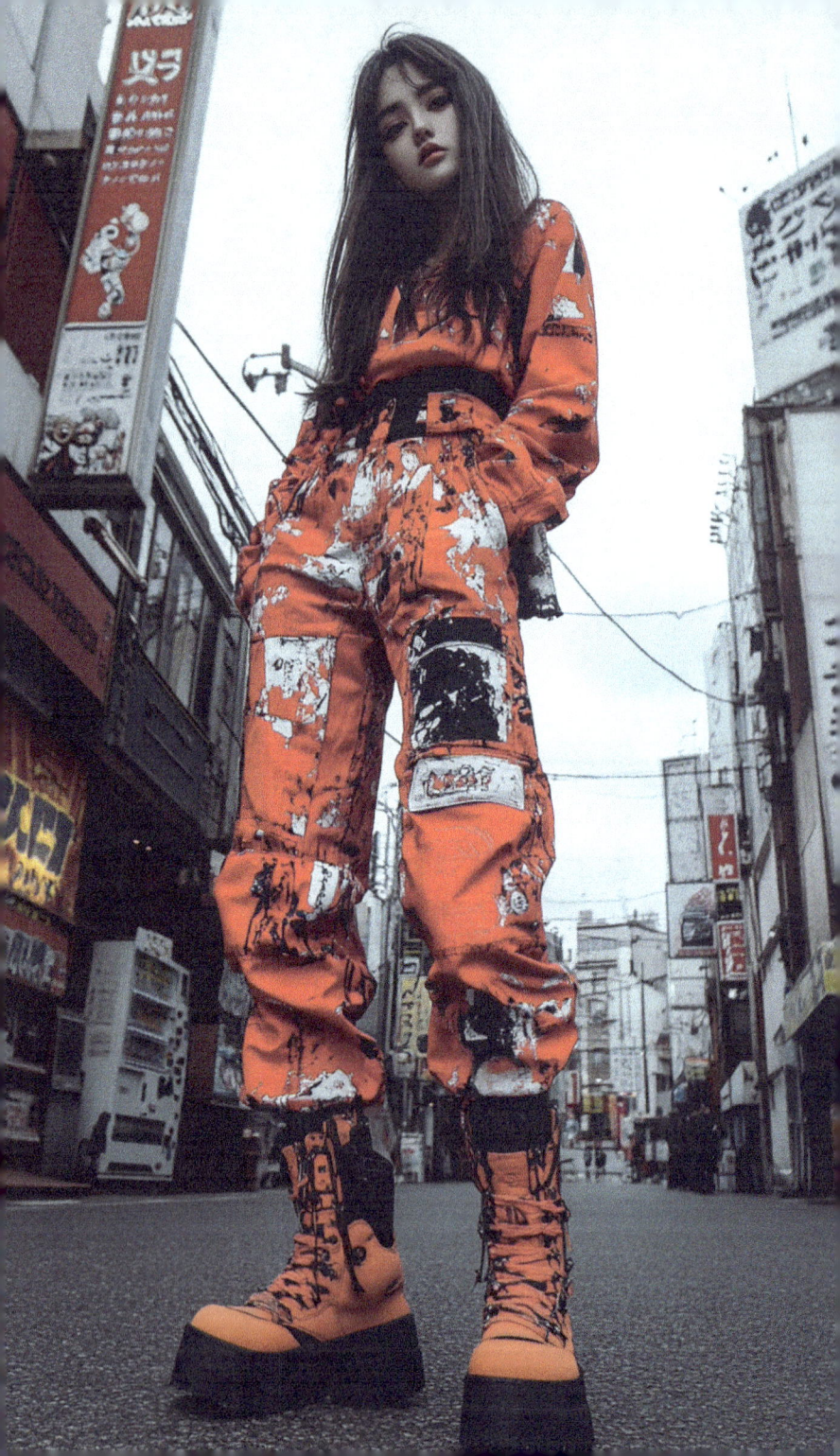

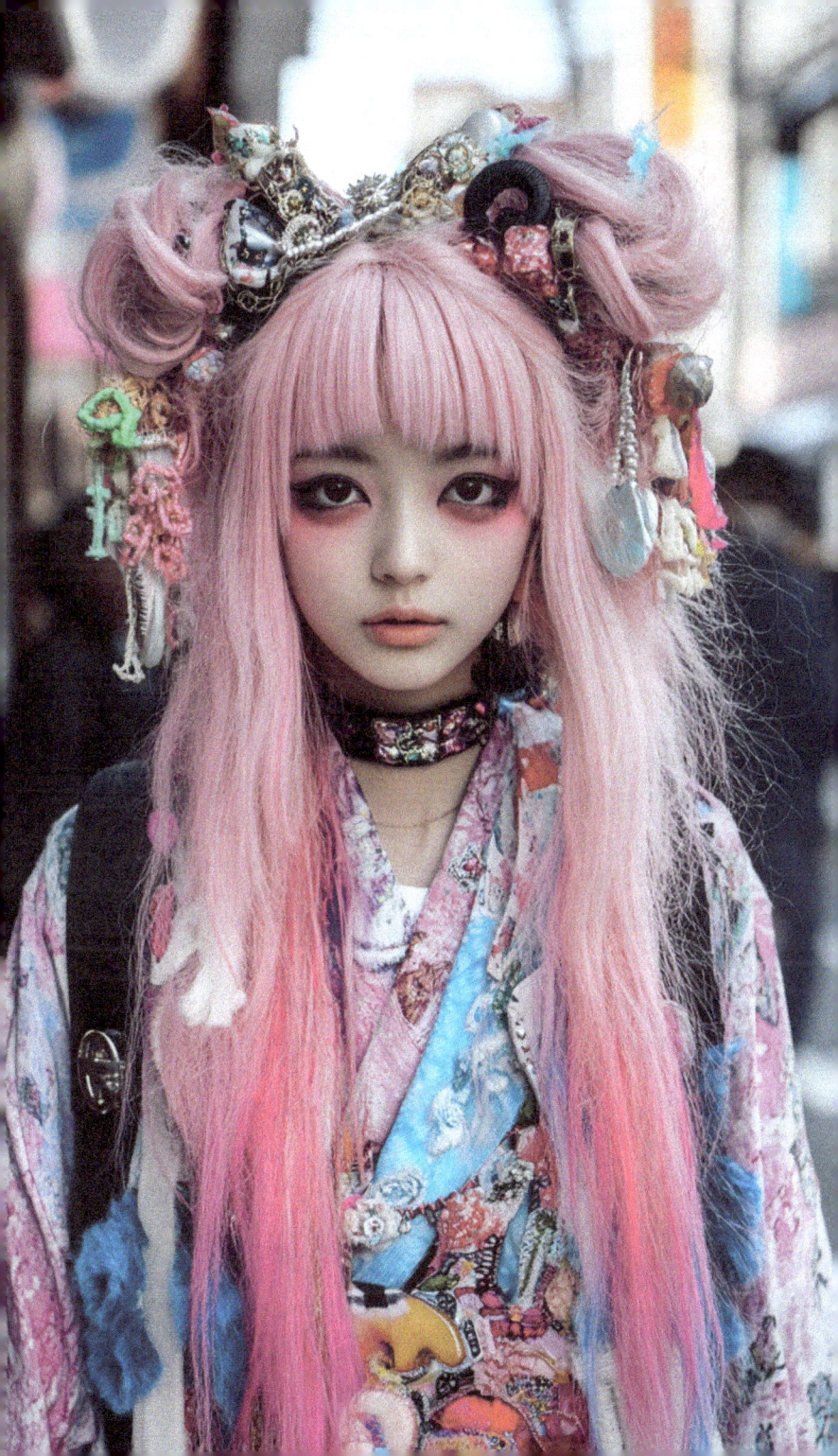

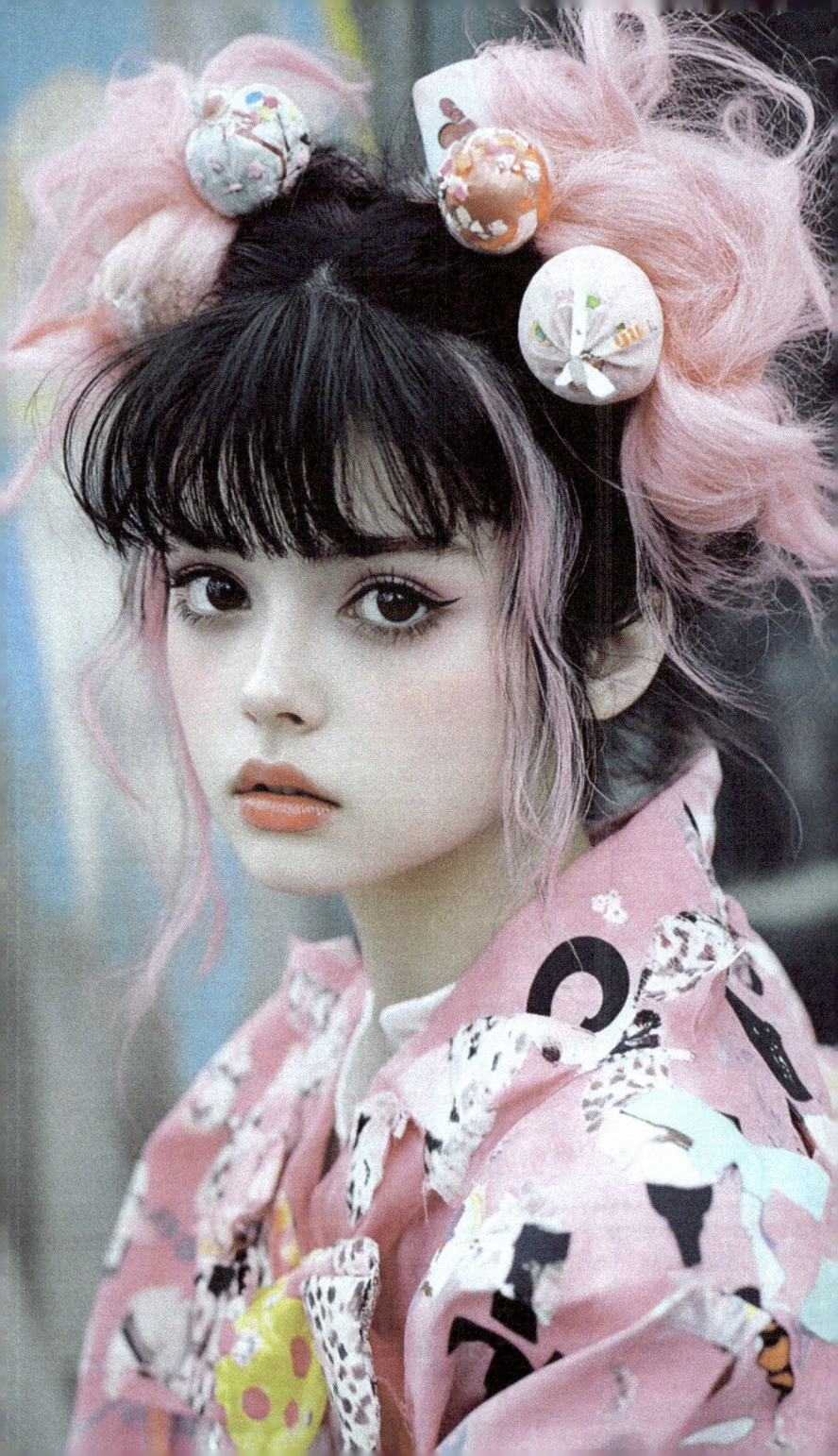

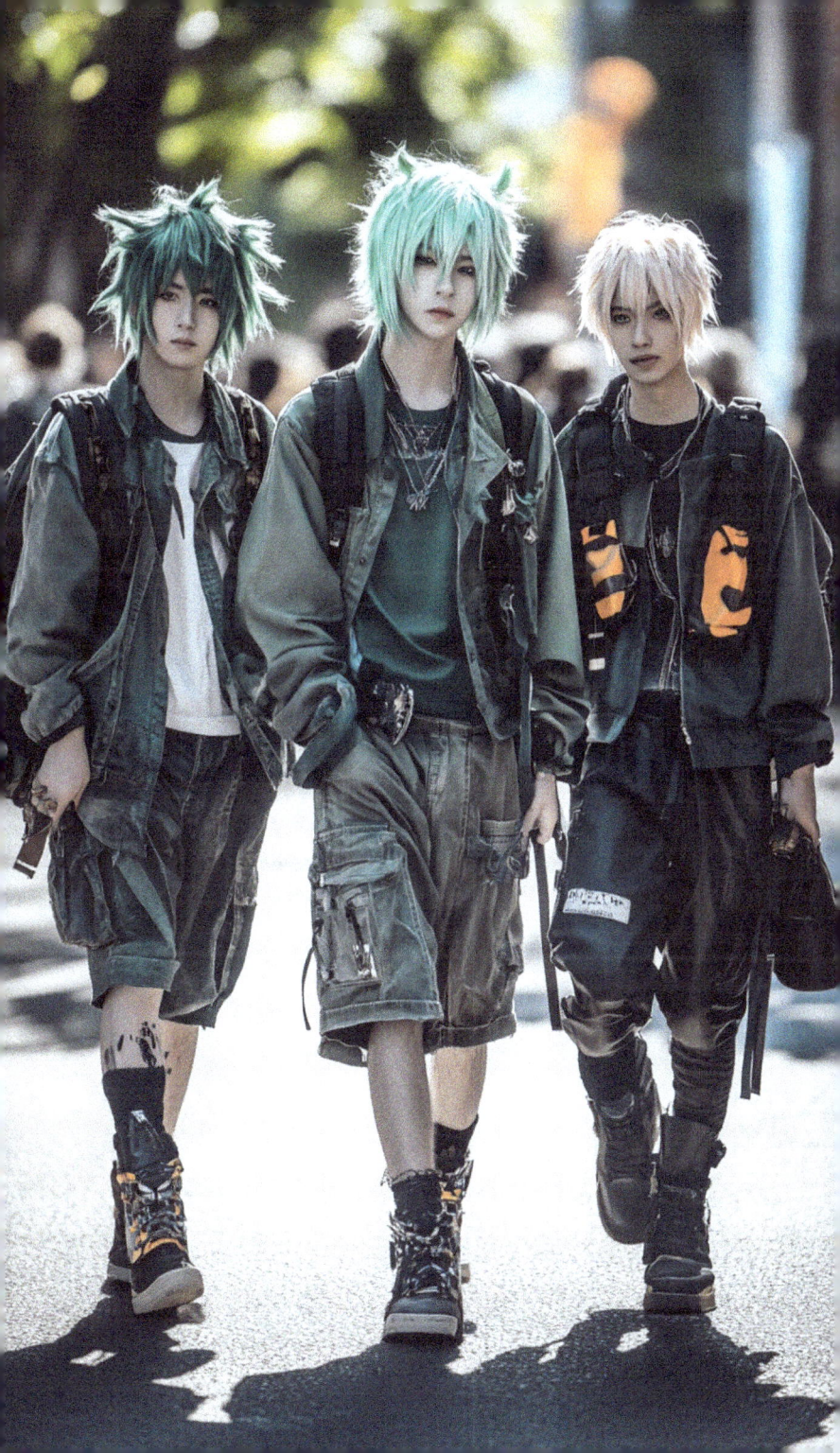

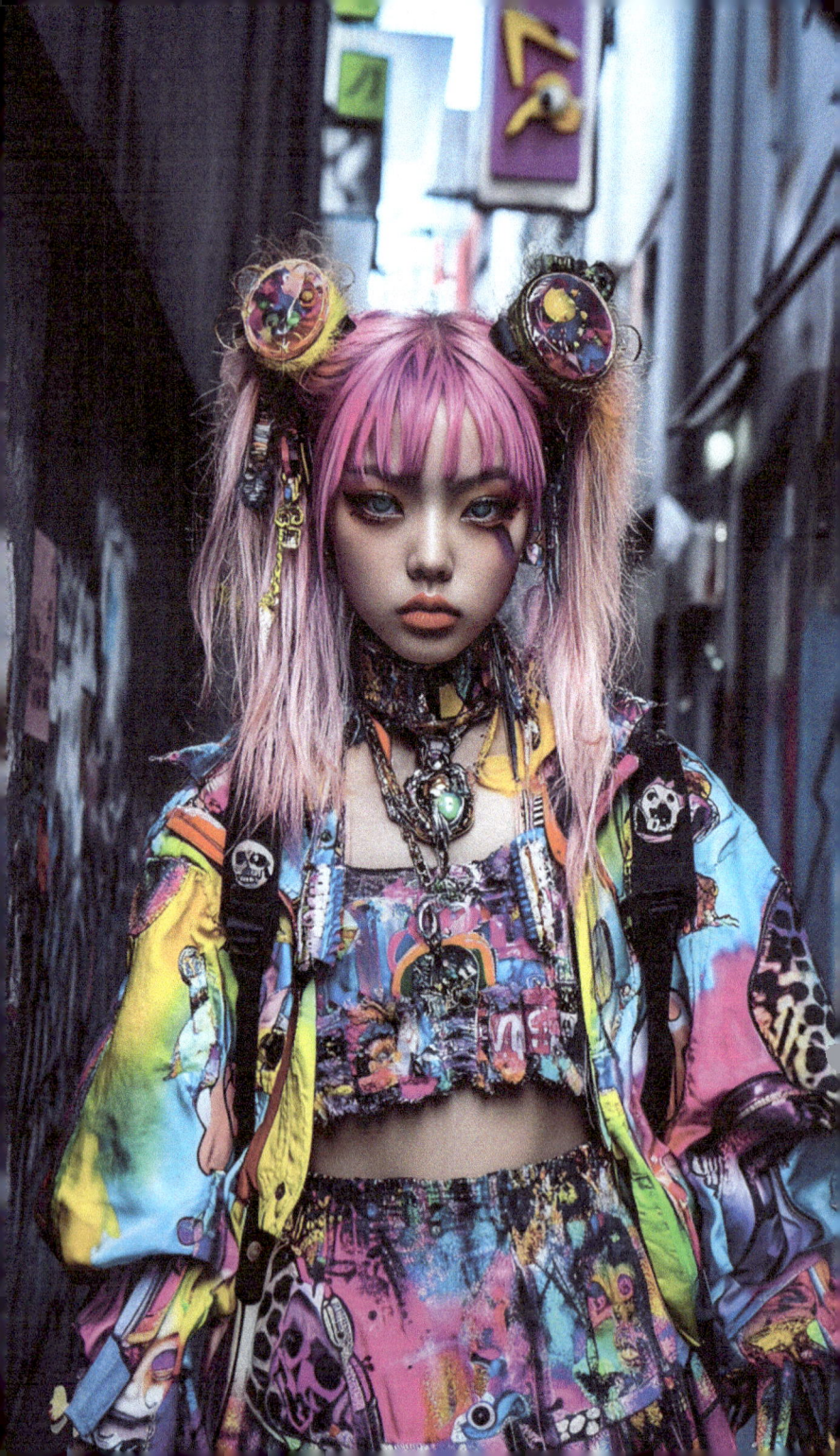

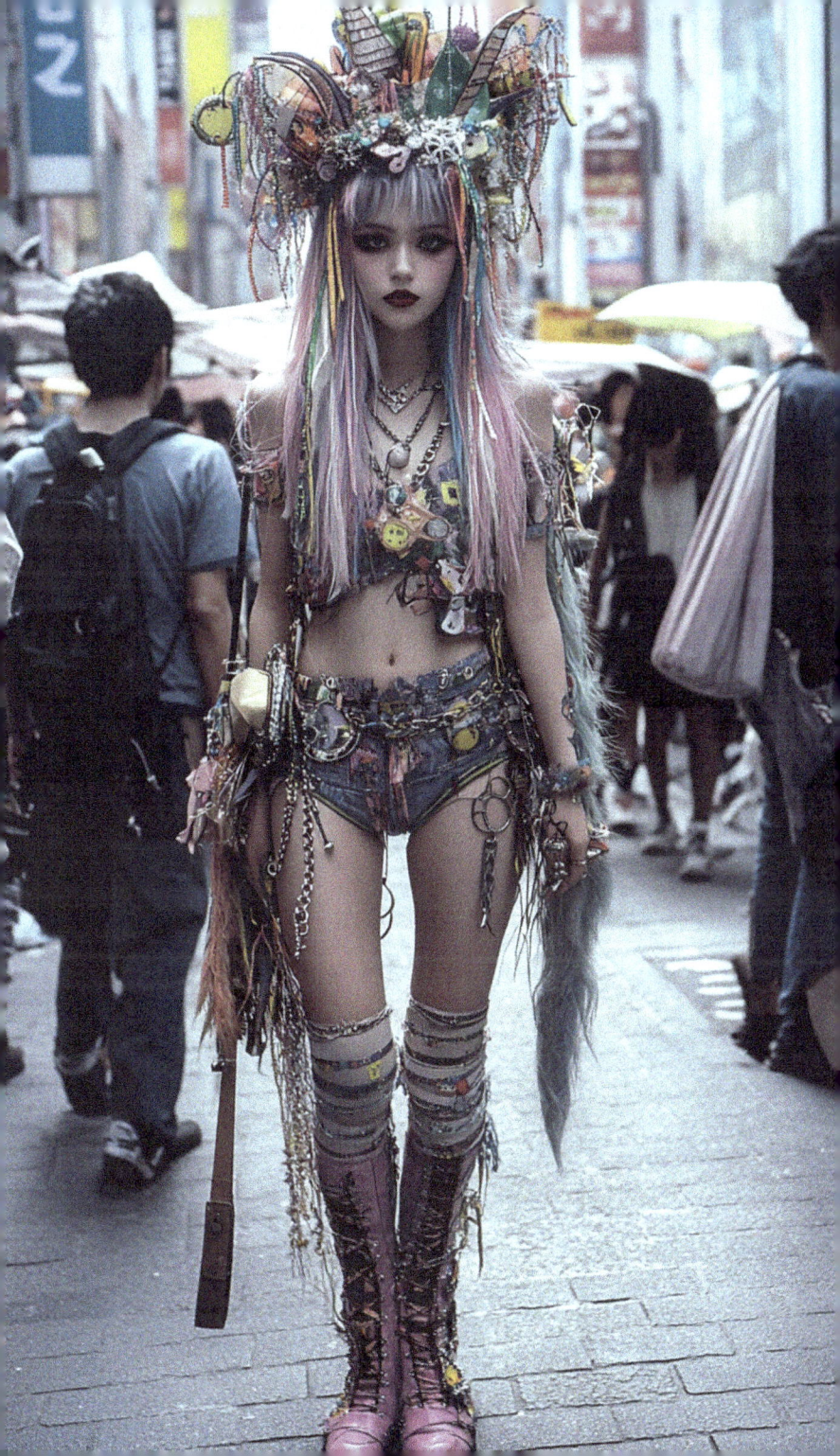

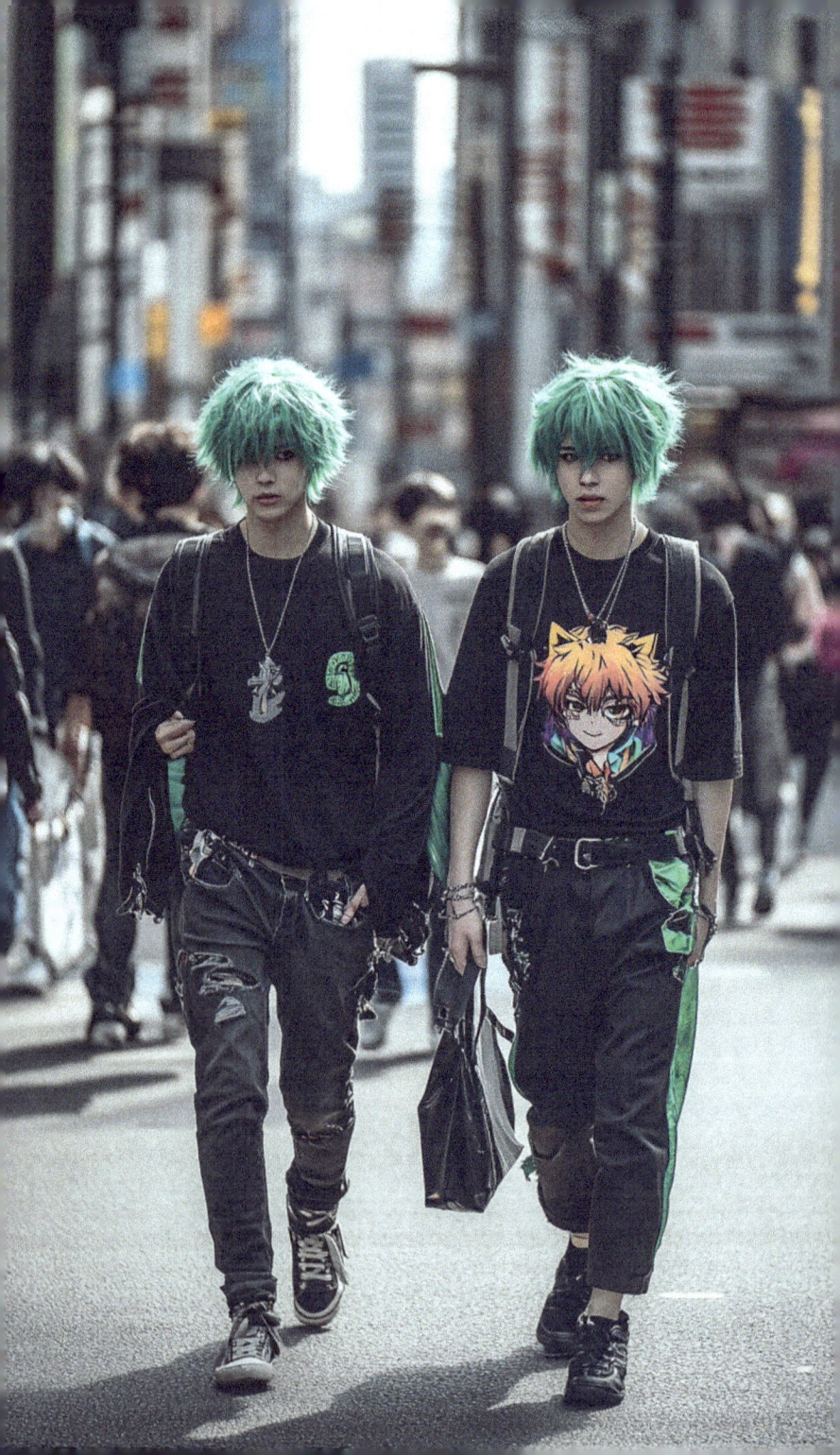

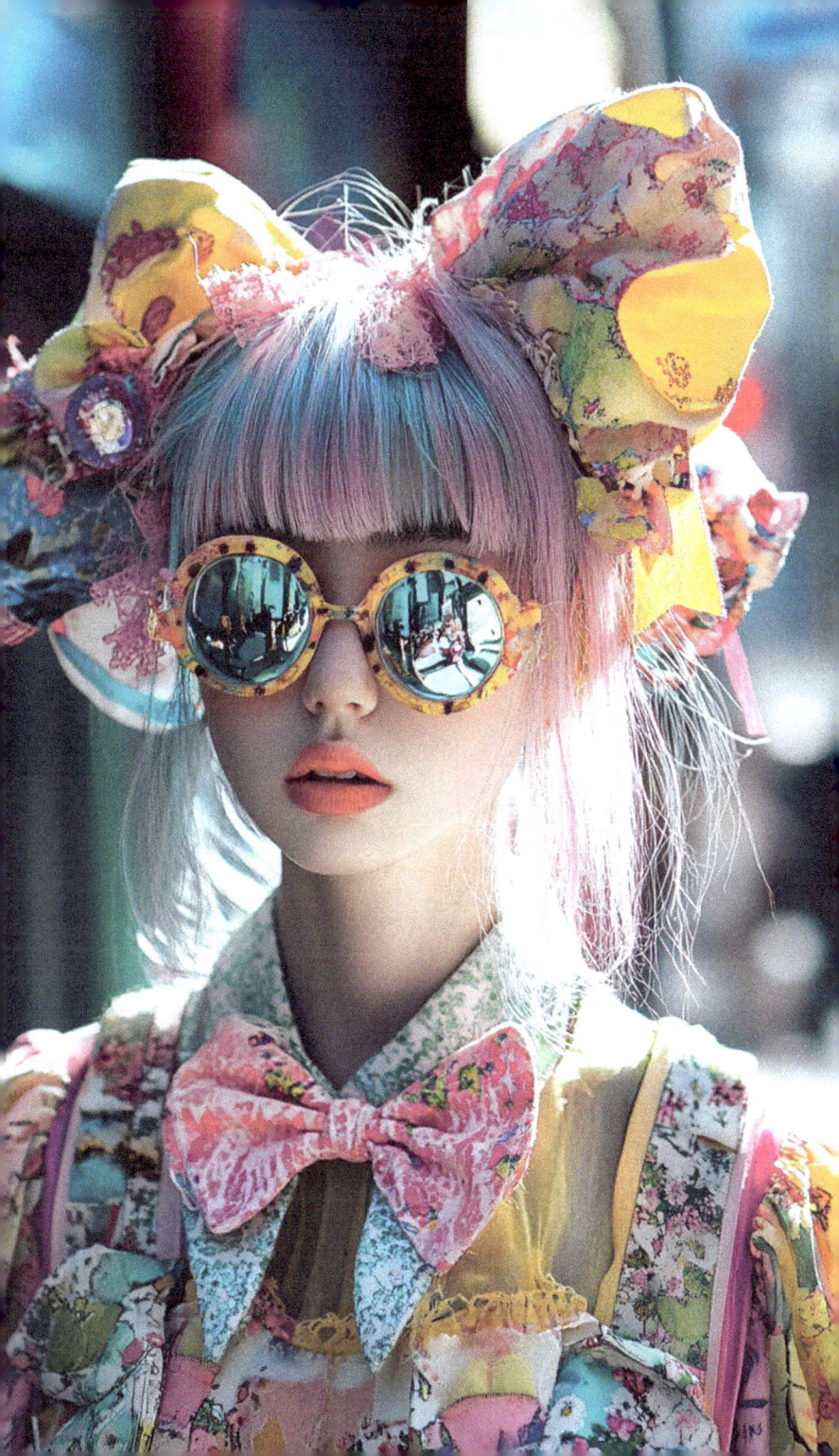

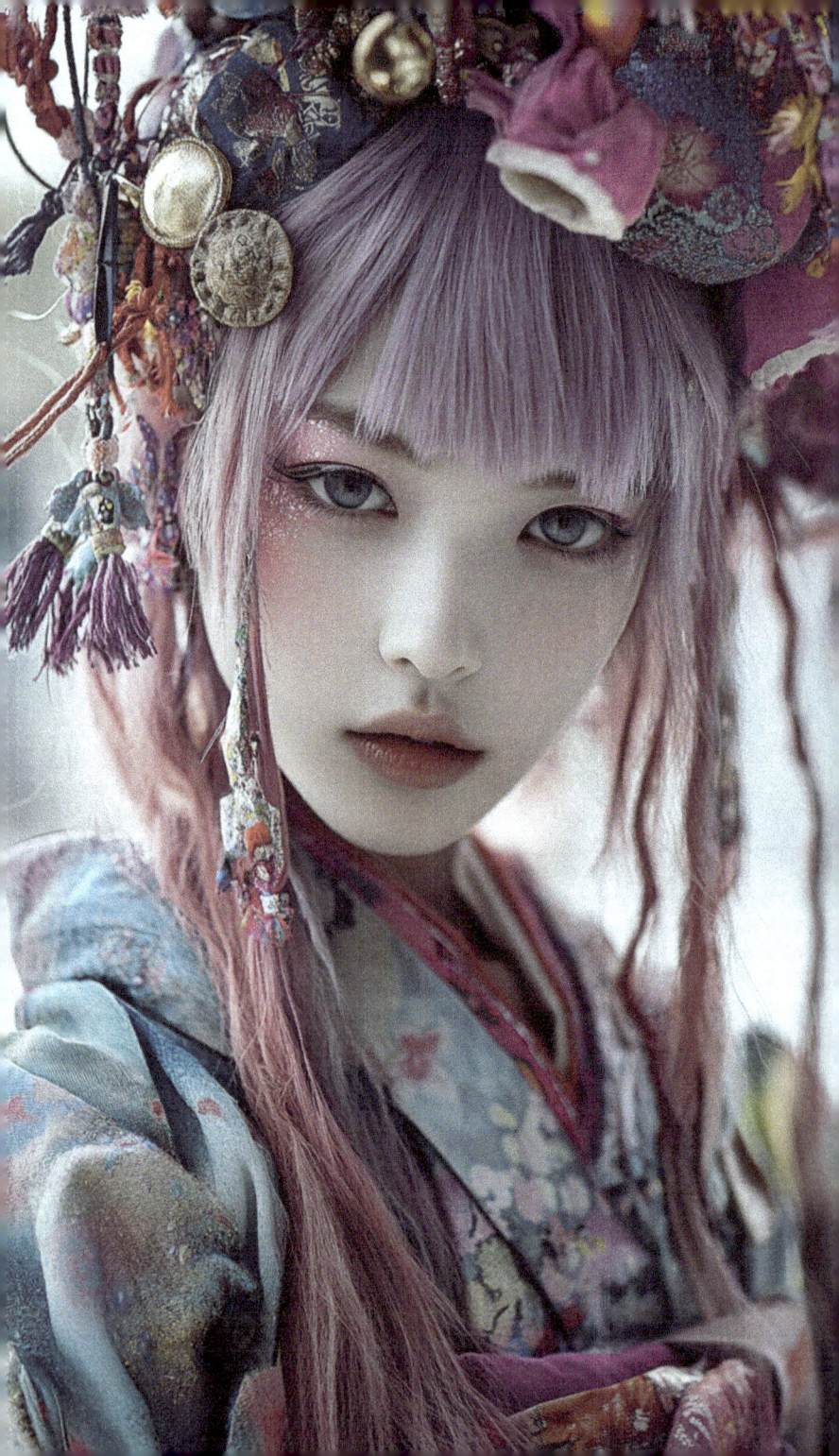

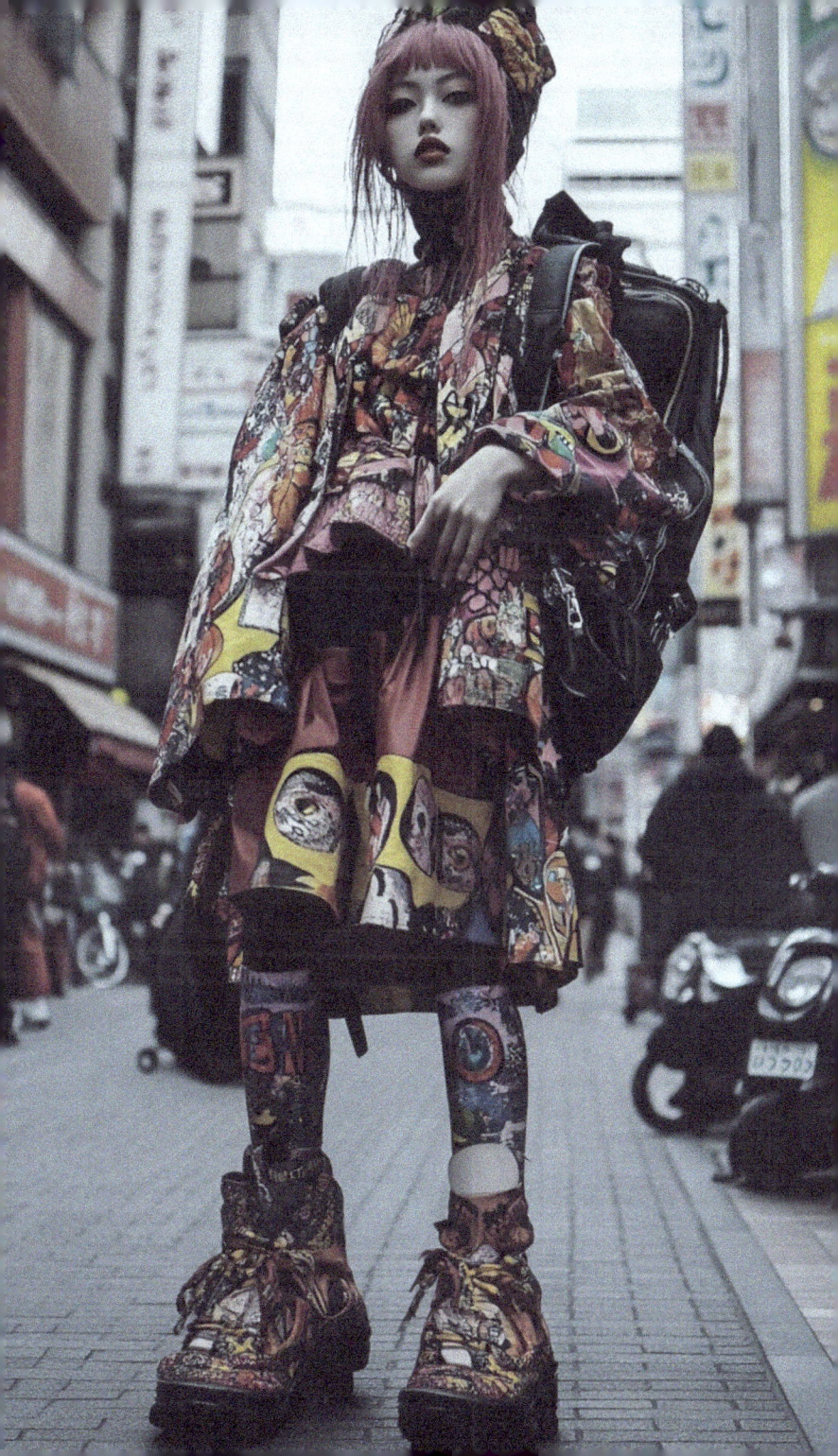

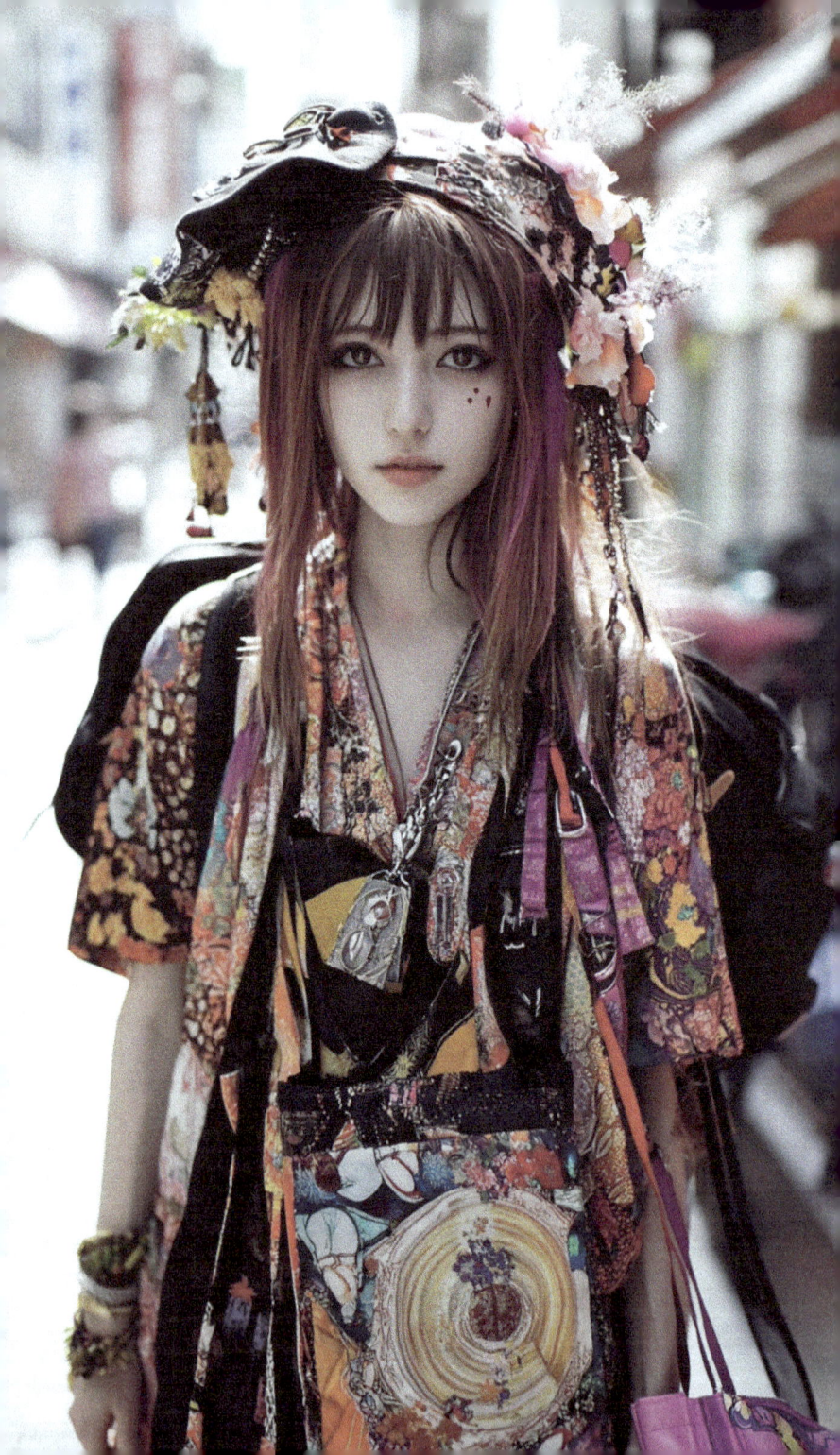

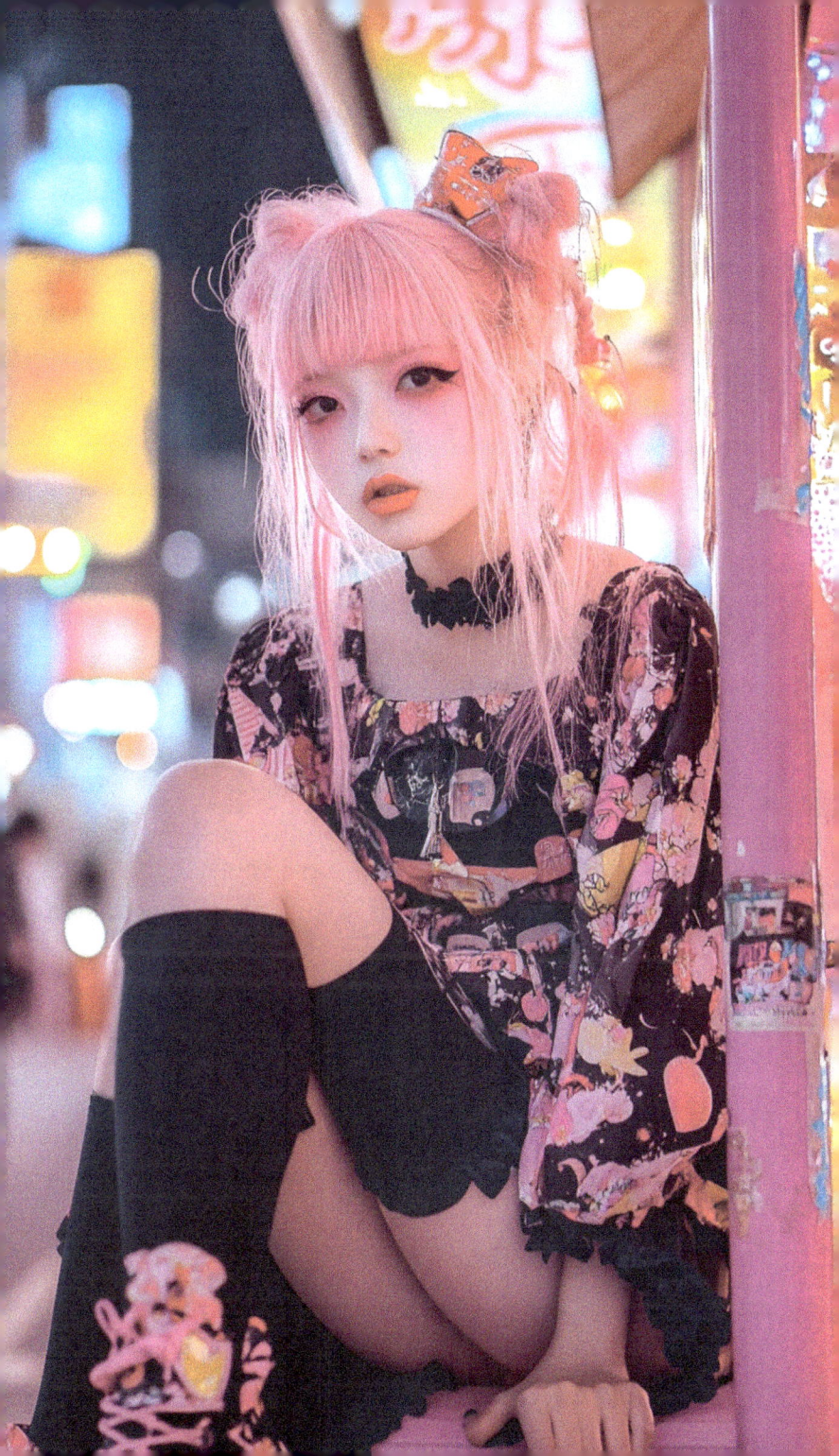

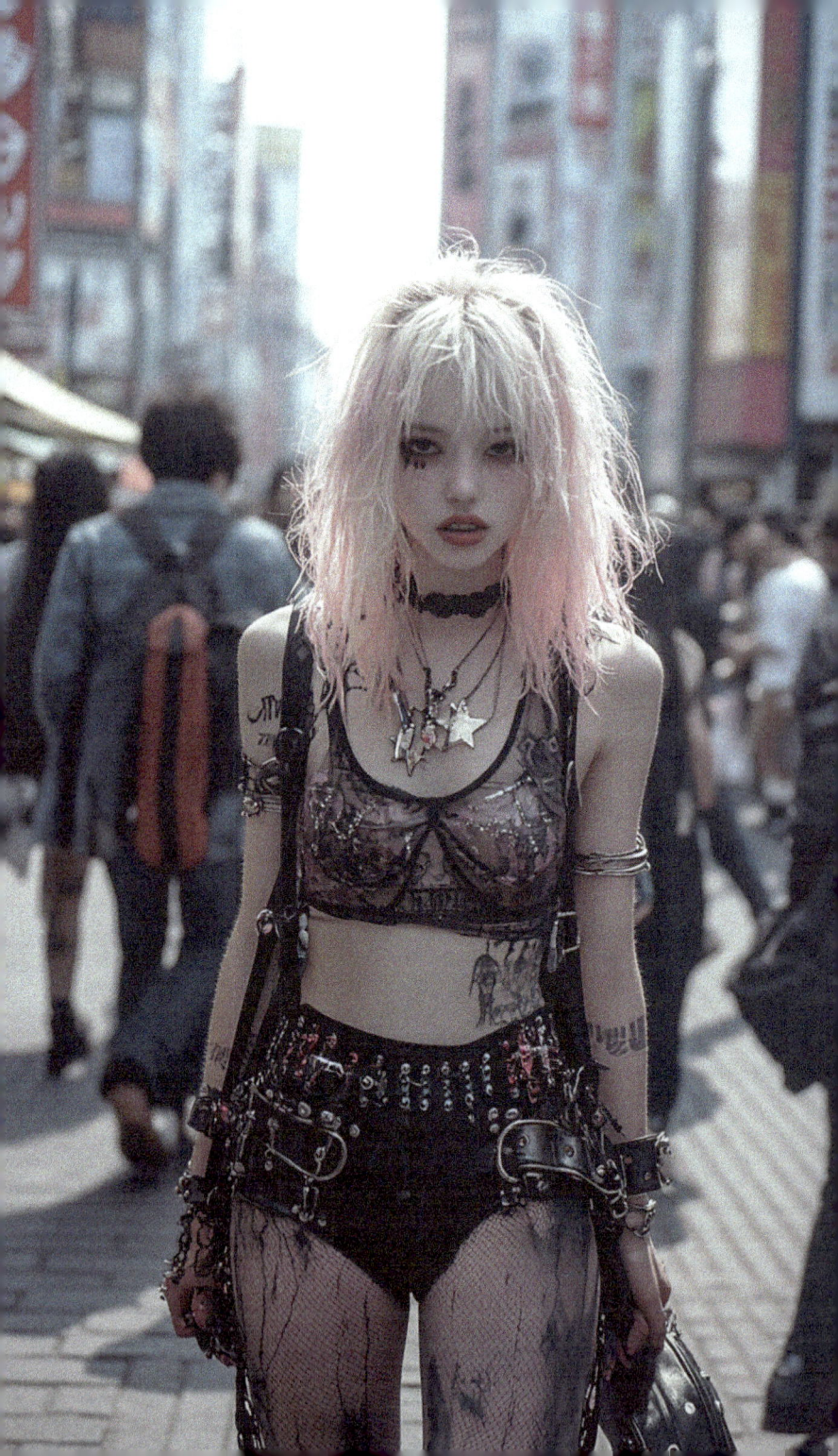

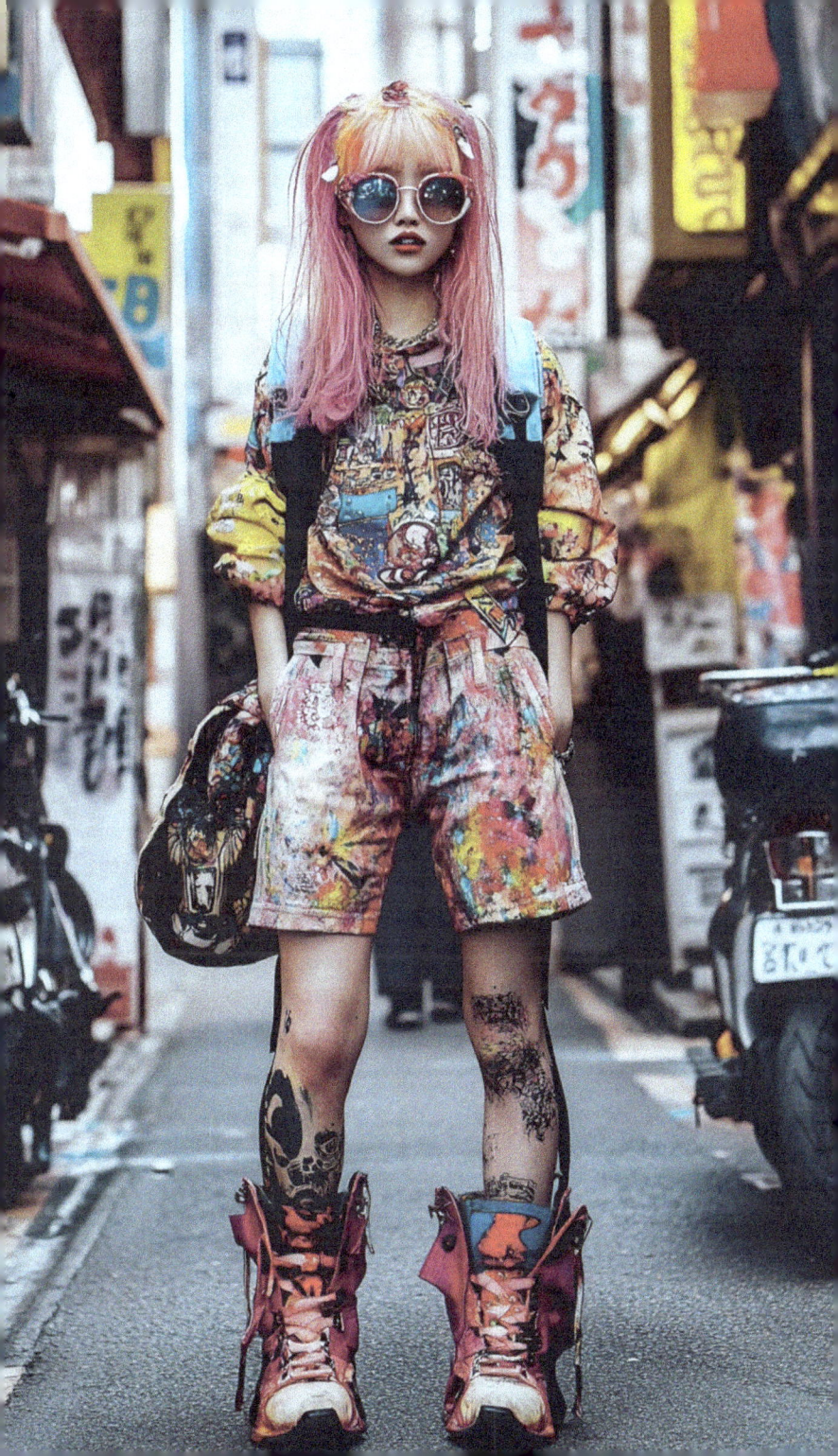

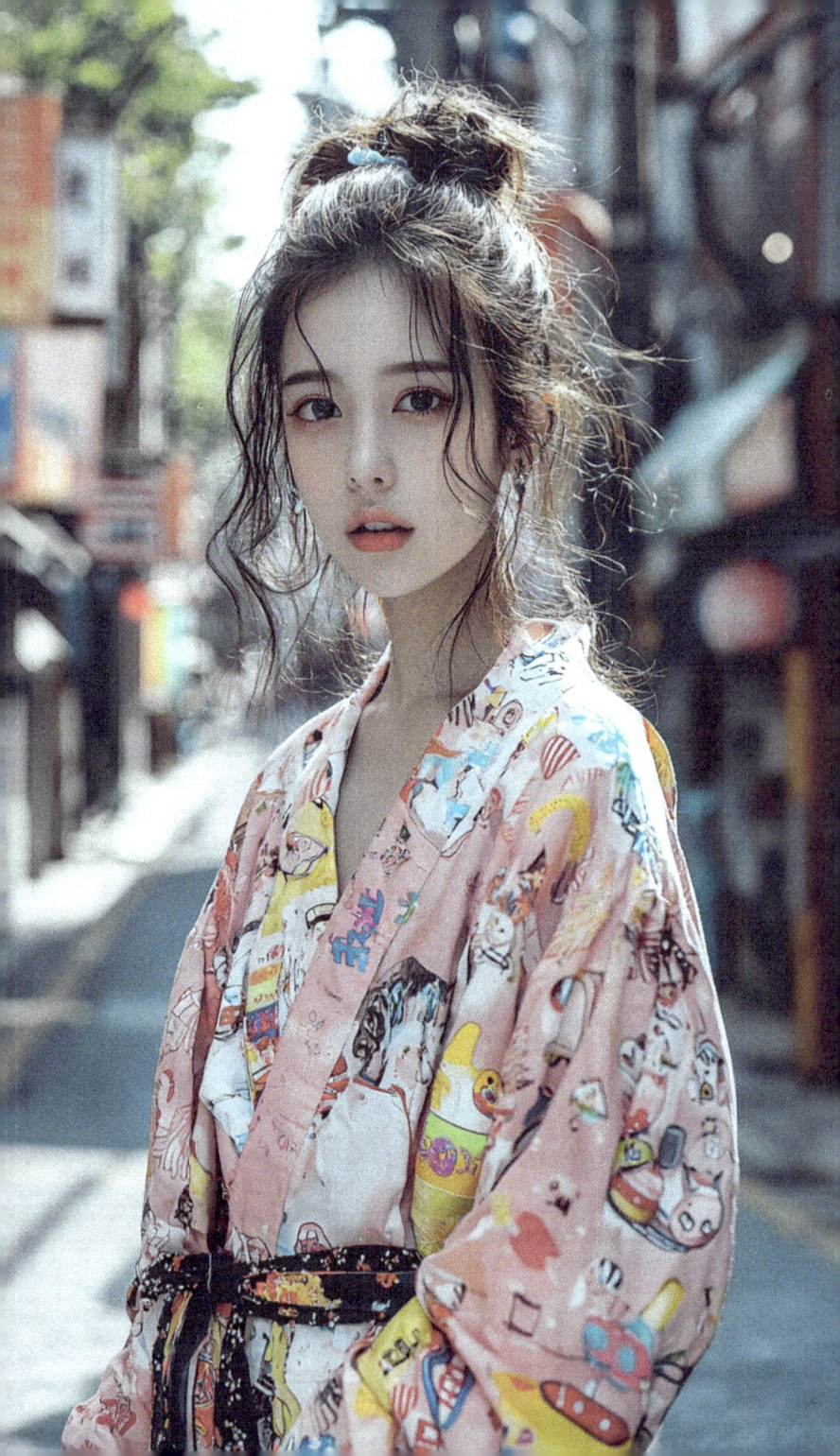

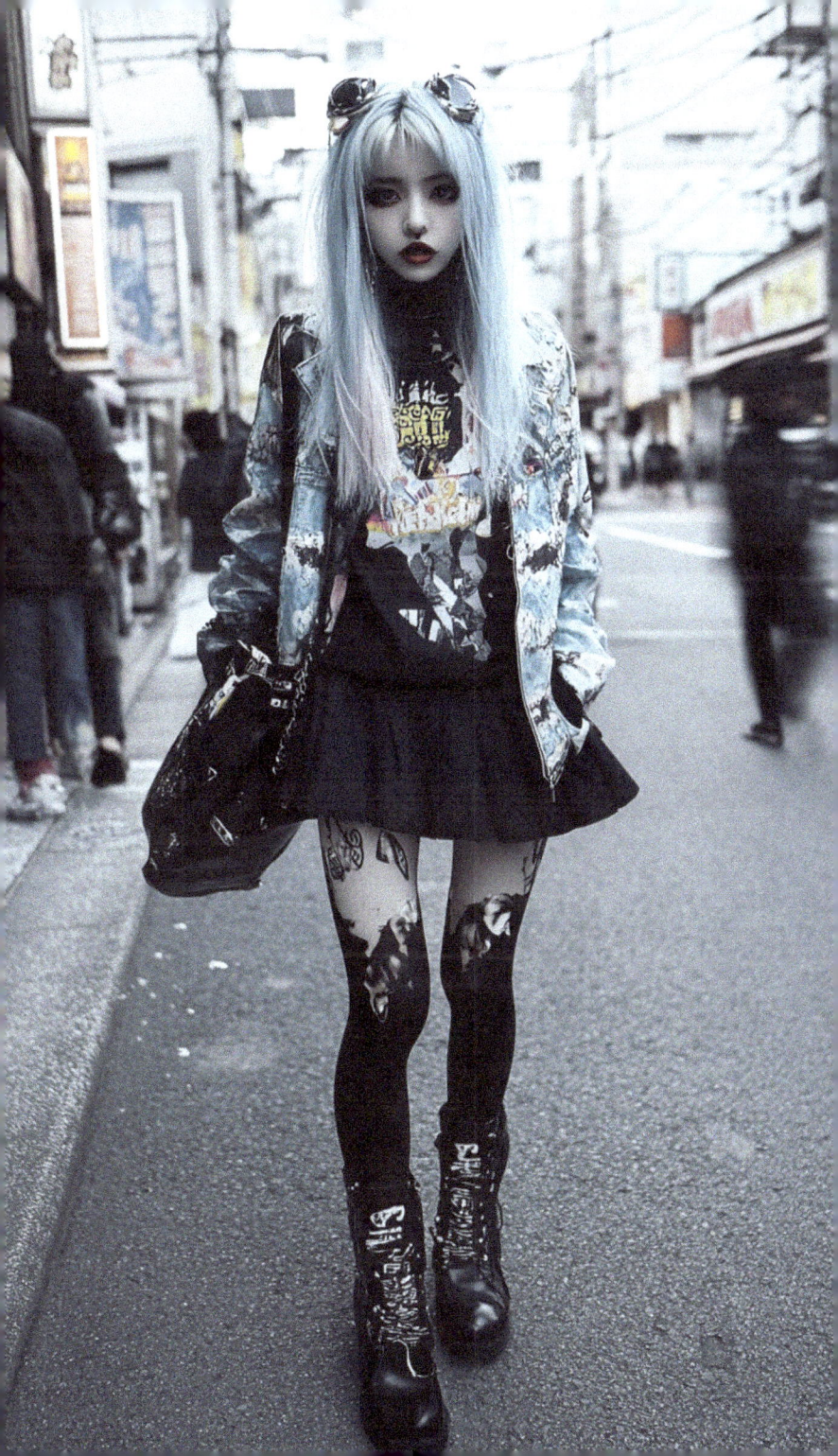

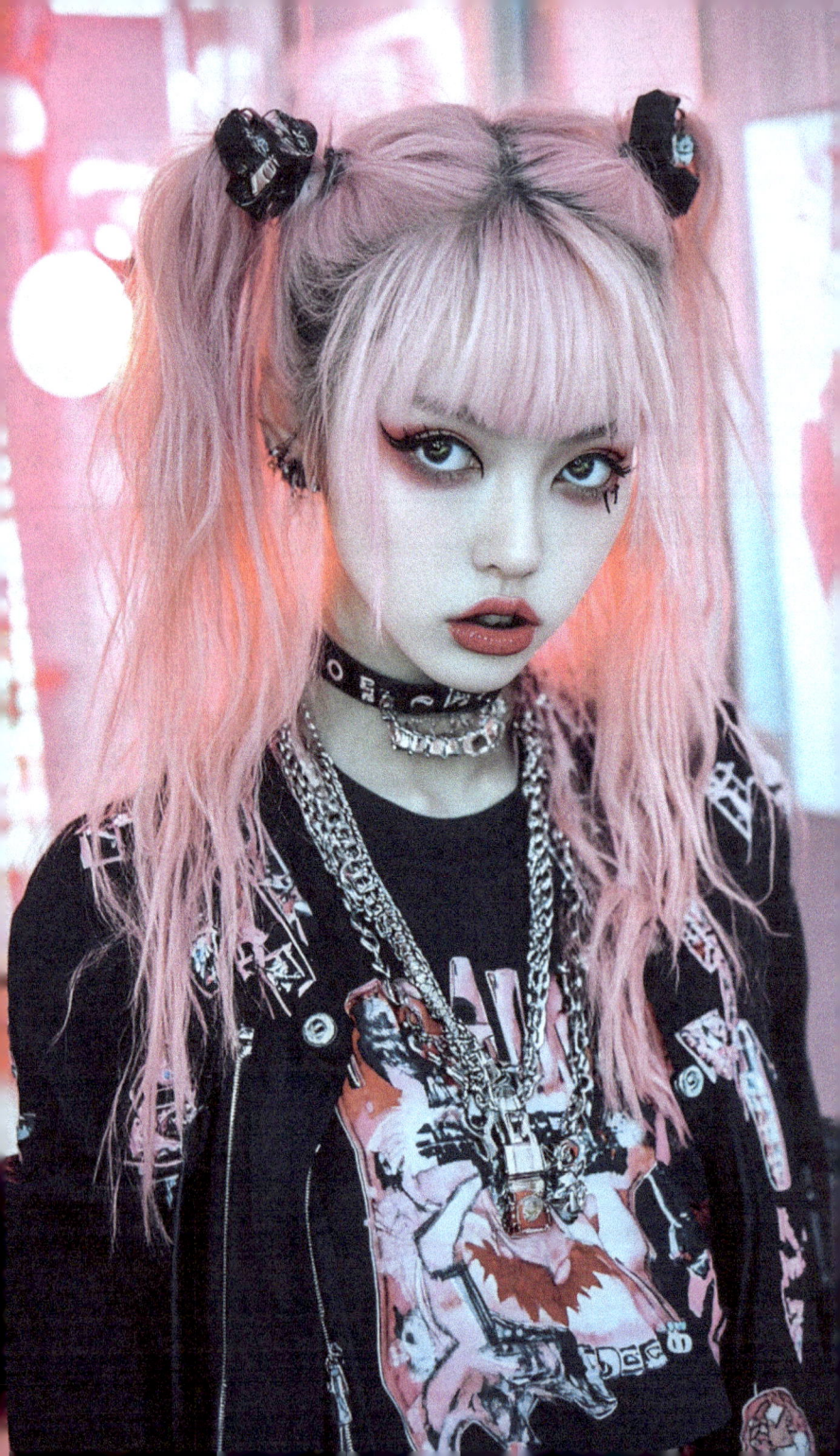

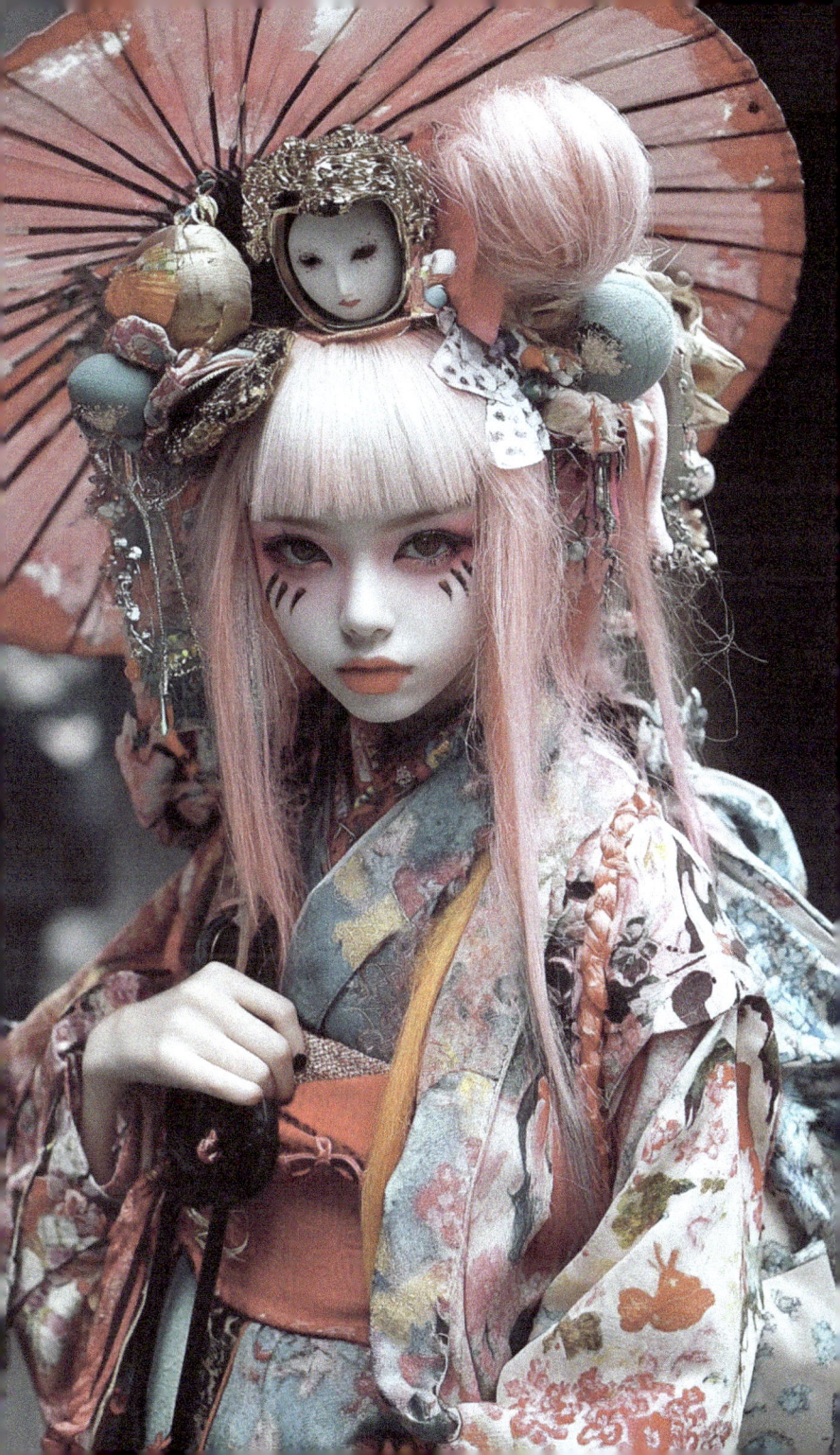

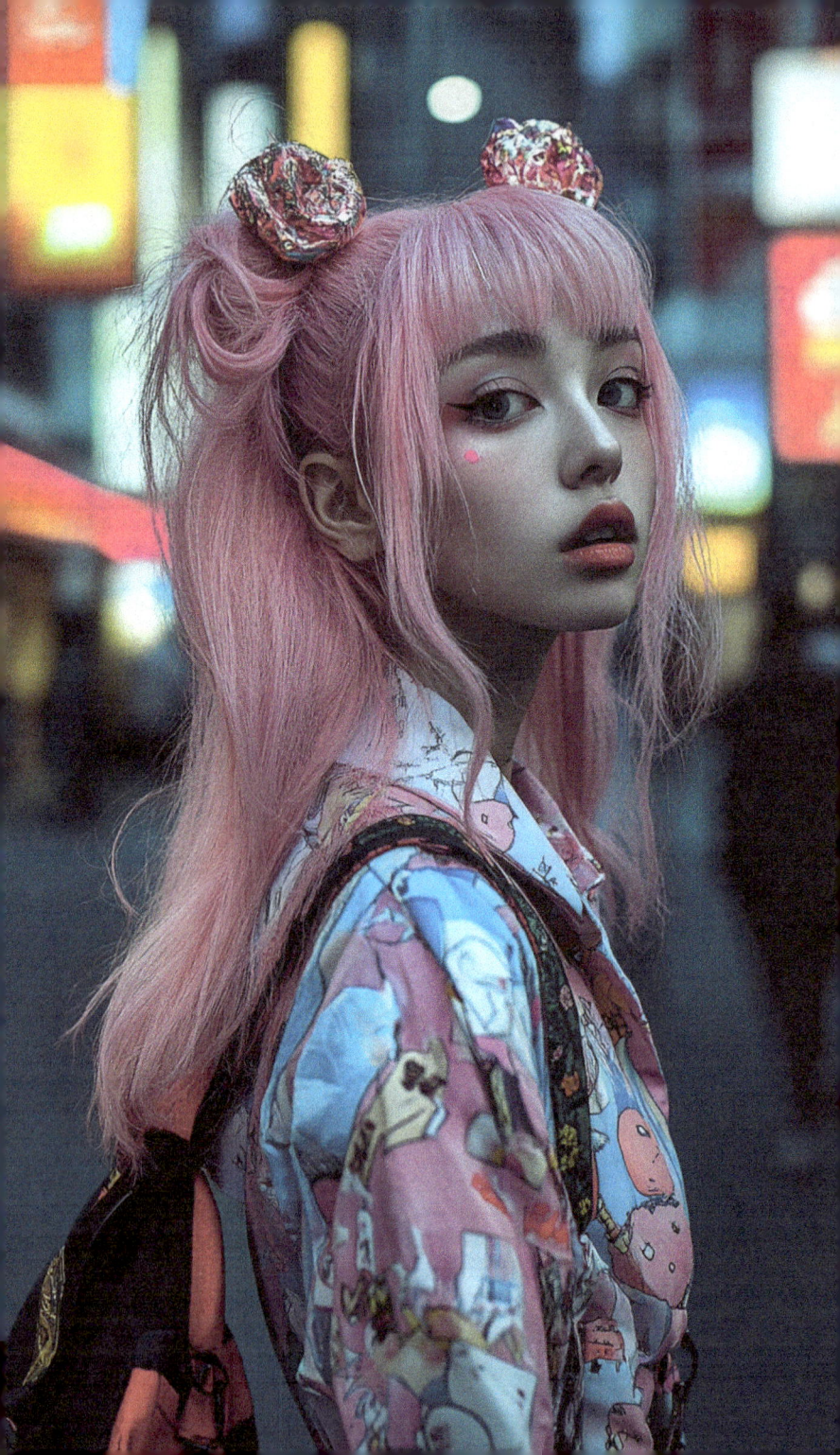

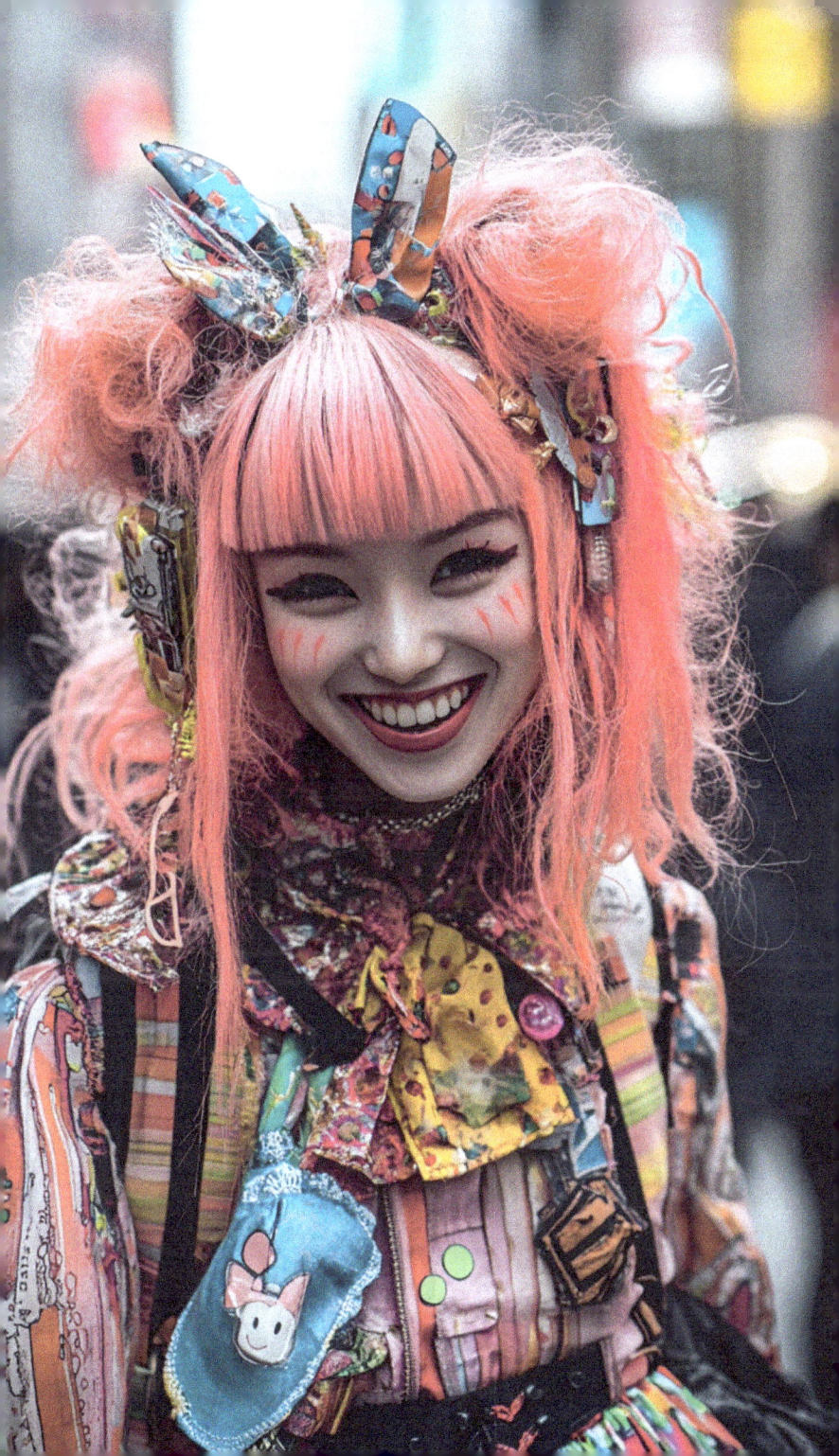

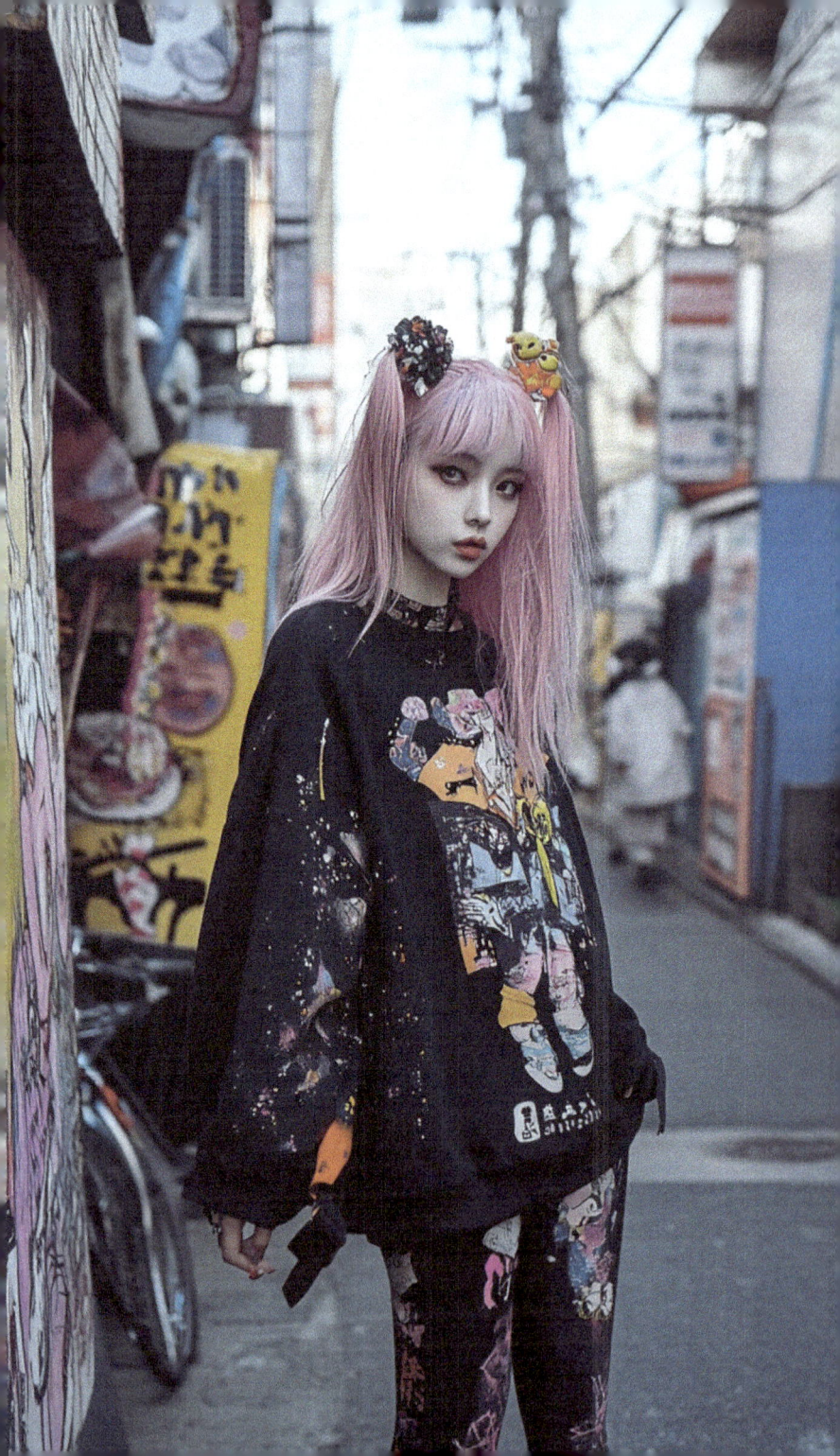

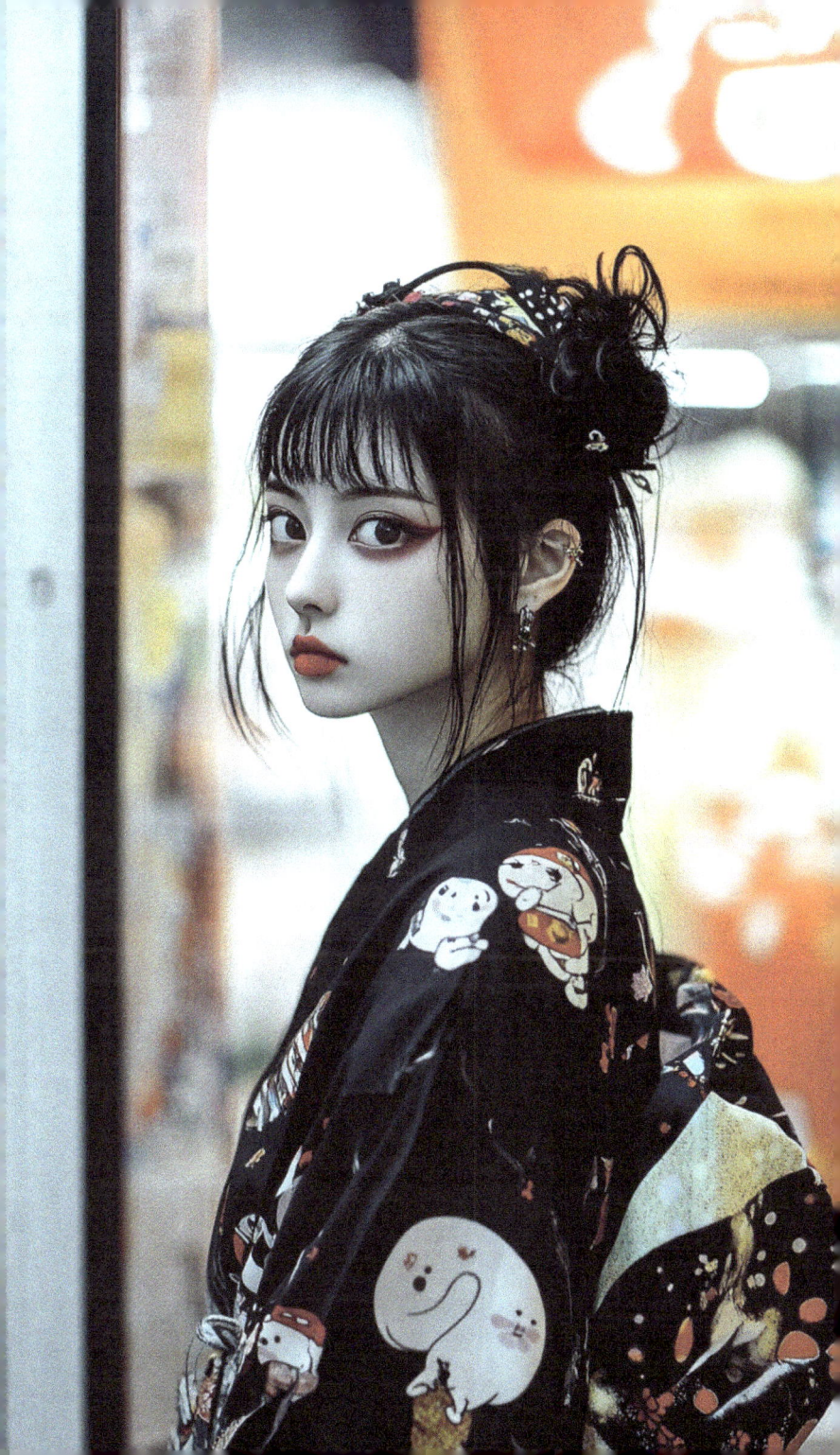

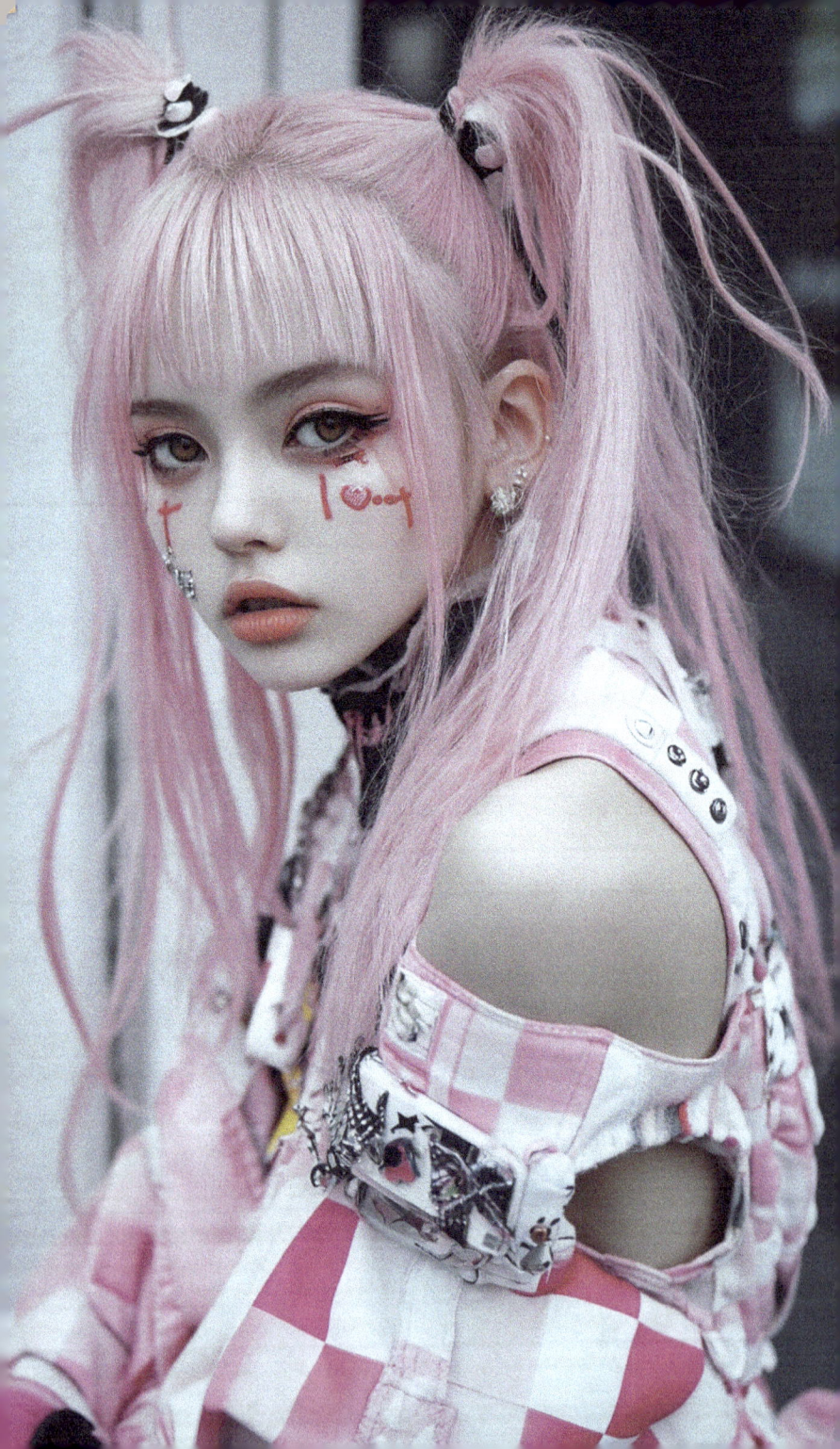

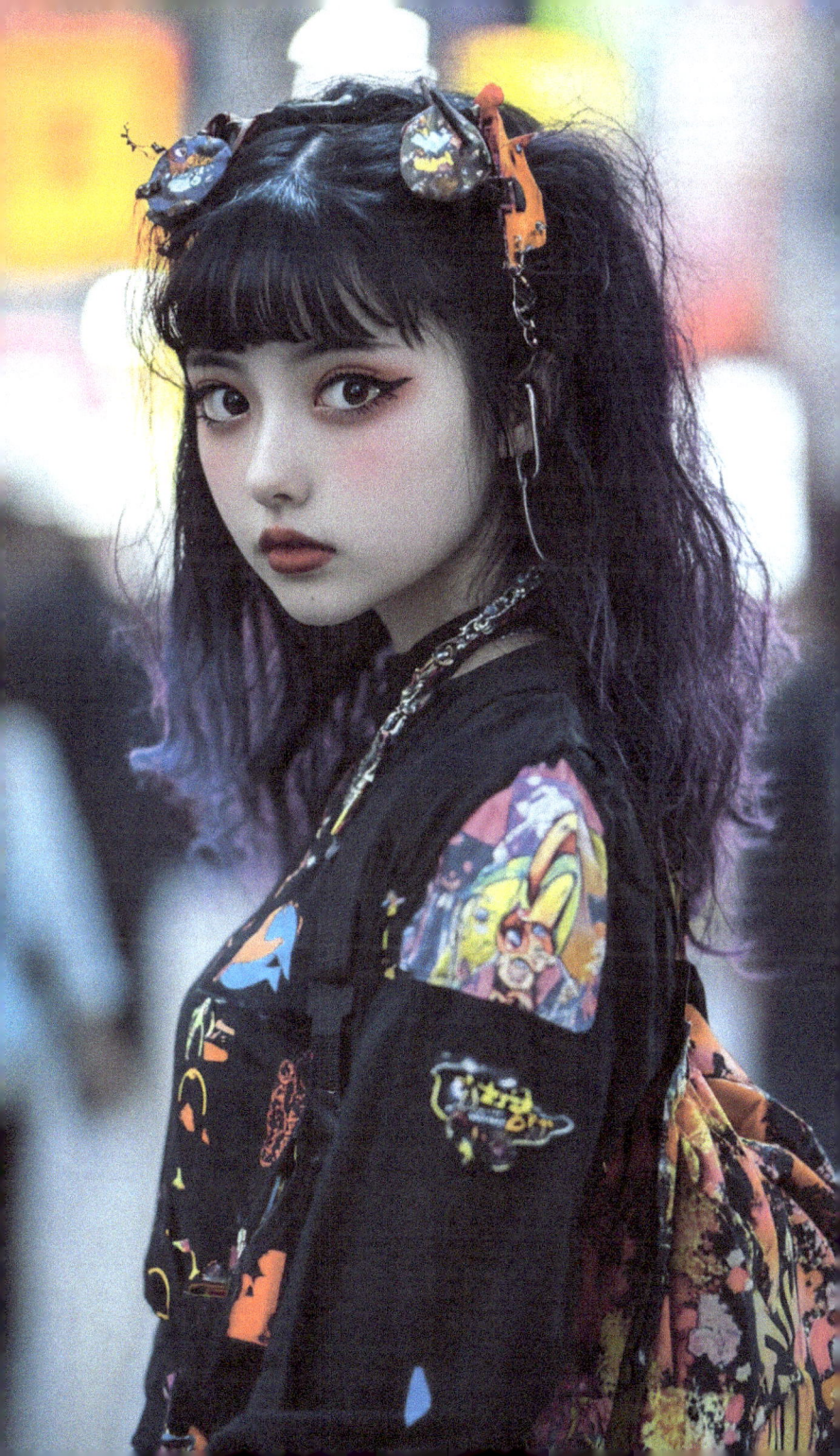

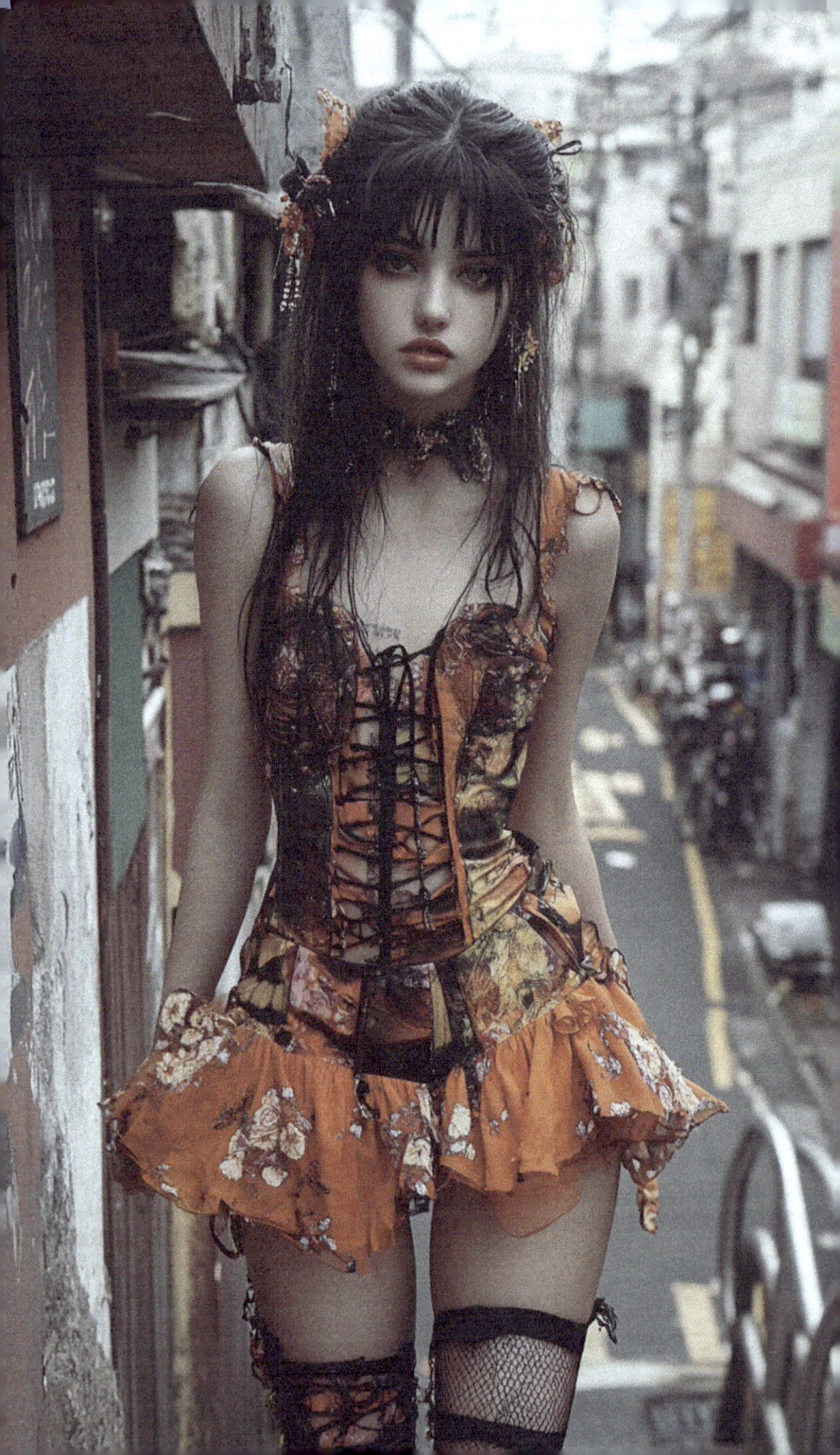

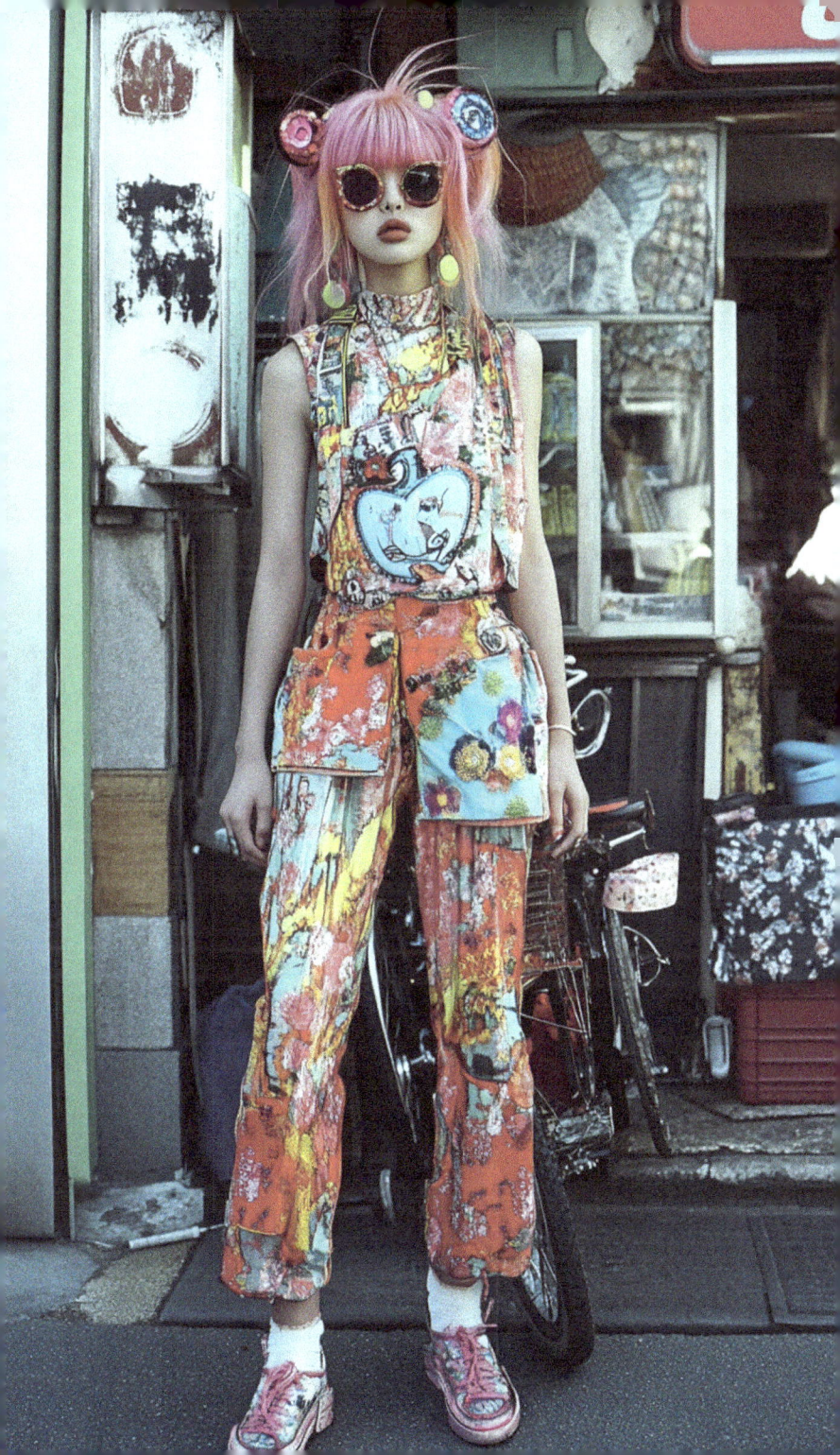

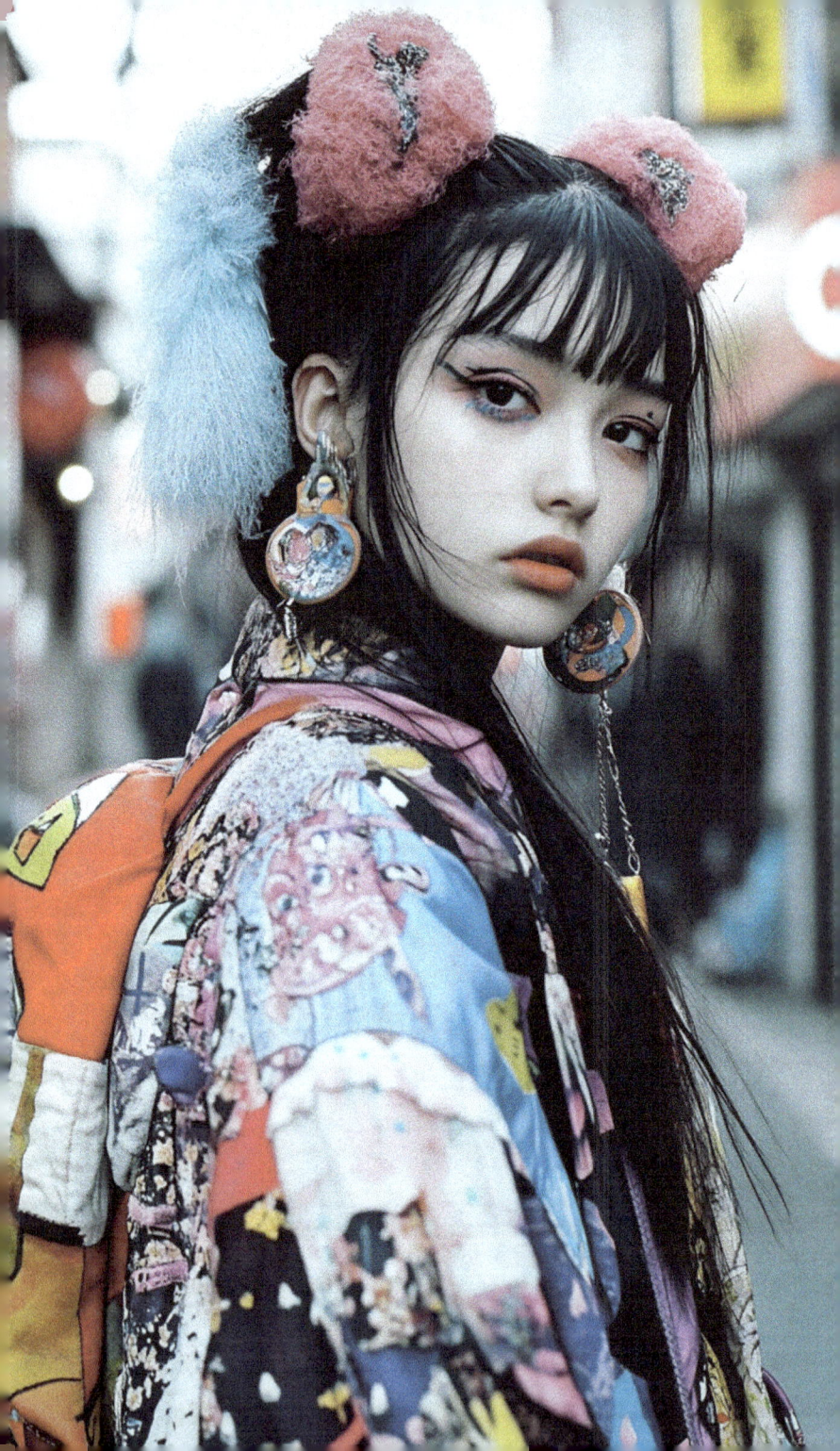

www.ingramcontent.com/pod-product-compliance
Lightning Source LLC
Chambersburg PA
CBHW070207230526
45471CB00002B/863